REDEDICATION

A STORY OF SEX, REPENTANCE AND RESTORATION

GODZCHILD PUBLICATIONS

© 2011 Godzchild, Inc.

Published by Godzchild Publications
a division of Godzchild, Inc.
22 Halleck St., Newark, NJ 07104
www.godzchildproductions.net

Printed in the United States of America 2011— First Edition
Book Cover designed by Ana Saunders of Es3lla Designs

Library of Congress Cataloging-in-Publications Data
Rededication: A Story of Sex, Repentance and Restora-
tion/Armond Mosley. Includes bibliographical references,
scriptural references and a workbook.

ISBN 978-1-937095-00-0 (pbk.)

1. Mosley, Armond. 2. Inspirational 3. Christianity
4. Religion 5. Encouragement

02011927696

TABLE OF CONTENTS

THE *Rededication* WORKBOOK

DEDICATION

To my lovely wife Nneka, the journey that follows is what led me to you. While there were many valleys along the way, the fact that the end result was my union to you makes the story worth remembering. I thank God each and every day for caring enough about me to bring us together. I love you and thank you so much for your undying love and support.

FOREWORD

*O*ne particular aspect of the Bible that has always intrigued me is the level of transparency that is on display. How men, inspired by God, exposed their frailties, mistakes, failures, idiosyncrasies, and conquests. I felt and sensed that same type of transparency as I read *Rededication* and it is what truly makes it a great read. *Rededication* forces us to step into our own memory bank of situations and relive those spiritually inconsistent moments. It is in this reflective state, that we are afforded the opportunity to correct some of our own mindsets and discover how God was actually speaking in that still, small voice, before, during and after each sexual encounter.

As I began to read *Rededication*, I started to remember my first time, second time, etc. Working through each chapter, I began to recall that flood of emotions I felt as a new believer; how I experienced feelings of remorse and the loving conviction of the Holy Spirit as a result of my own sexual indiscretions. Immediately, I wanted to call everyone I could remember and apologize for what I had encouraged them to do. Twenty-six years ago, this was my moment of repentance and the beginning of God's restorative process in my life. I pray that as you read Armond's story, that you will have a moment of revelation, a moment of inspiration and a moment of edification that will launch you into your own journey of rededication.

This book is a "clarion call" to all who are outside the entity of marriage. My heart grieves as this generation moves further away from God's original intent of fruitfulness and multiplication. I believe that this book is timely in its direct approach to candidly and transparently deal with the issue of faith and sexuality. No matter where you are in your own journey, I am confident that you will find relevance in the pages that follow. My prayer is that, as you read this book, the voice and love of the Holy Spirit will flood your spirit and soul. I pray that as the Holy Spirit illuminates your mind, your stance and position on celibacy will be strengthened and that the promise of the Father will be yours according to Ephesians 5:28-29 which says, [28] *"So husbands ought to love their own wives as their own bodies; he who loves his wife loves himself. [29] For no one ever hated his own flesh, but nourishes and cherishes it, just as the Lord does the church"* manifest in your marriage. That is the promise that, **"you can experience heaven on earth in your marriage."** The grace and favor of waiting, positions you to experience a relationship in marriage that exemplifies Heaven on earth.

Peace and Blessings,
Pastor Louis G. Whiting

DISCLAIMER

The names of some of the characters within have been changed to protect the identities of those involved.

REDEDICATION

INTRODUCTION

Galatians 5:13 – "You, my brothers, were called to be free. But do not use your freedom to indulge the sinful nature; rather, serve one another in love."

$\mathscr{I}$think we have all felt the repressive guilt within resulting from the burden of sin. I often questioned if it was subconsciously manufactured or truly what I heard many times before called the "Holy Spirit's guiding hand" on my life. After all, most of the situations where I felt this nudging and internal pricking were not unique to those encountered by anyone else in my peer circle and yet, I never heard them speak of any form of sincere guilt. In fact, at times, it seemed as if they reveled in those very same moments that I found extremely discomforting. It is possible, however, that the origins of the discomfort I felt may have resulted from the inundation of sermons on sexual immorality that I grew up listening to, which planted seeds in me that were finally beginning to take root in my life. Whatever the case, I had come to realize on this particular evening no matter how hard I tried to rationalize or justify it, I would not be able to block out the voice of God.

As our bodies aligned in perfect symmetry, she and I laid there in the throes of spiritual inconsistency prepared to embark on what was anticipated to be a most sensually fulfilling adventure. With that expectation in mind, our journey began with a customary thrust and a mutually obligatory contraction. This back and forth chess match continued on and on with an anxious energy; ever so often changing in intensity and alignment to create a more shared experience. As the pace increased and the moans grew louder, my body began to tense up in a convulsionary fashion and before long the stark pause where all worries would seem to disappear had arrived; and at that moment I passionately fought to regain control, but it was too late. With a sigh of relief and subsequent gasps for air, our journey toward ecstasy had come to a satisfyingly abrupt end.

Most times I would lay there with my head wedged in her bosom, but this time I felt the urgent need to get up. As I gathered myself, I looked down at her in admiration of God's perfect work – a woman. Truthfully, as I recount the day, I am not sure if I were in amazement at her sheer beauty or the beauty of the act of sex itself, but either way I stood there momentarily in awe. After a few minutes, my breathing had returned to a normal pace and when I peered down at her again she laid there as still as a baby in its crib fast asleep. I thought to myself, "job well done," but before I could savor the moment, the unbiased reality of what occurred quickly began to set in. Immediately my heart became heavy as I made my way out of the bedroom towards the bathroom. I heard a voice in my head say, "My son, you know better." I tried feverishly to shake what I believed was a subconsciously contrived ploy to ruin my moment, but I was unsuccessful. The voice grew louder and louder in my head until eventually, I found myself face to face with an image that was not immediately recognizable. It did not take long until I realized that I was standing in front of the bathroom mirror looking at my own reflection. Though my own reflection, there was something different about the individual in the mirror. He was not who I inherently believed *I* was. Sure, we had the same physical characteristics, but he represented an empowered caricature of one of my most desired sin areas; a caricature that I had been eagerly fighting to suppress for much of my adult life. But, on this fateful evening he had won and I had lost. As he eventually faded to black, the burden of the sin committed remained and I was left to carry it.

> ...but he represented an empowered caricature of one of my most desired sin areas; a caricature that I had been eagerly fighting to suppress for much of my adult life.

That was Fall 2006, when I once again fought against God and his commandment of sexual purity by way of sexual intercourse. I had tried before to submit to God and live a life of celibacy until marriage, but it was hard. Hard because so many others around me were doing the very thing I was trying to abstain from. Hard because as a young adult, sex and the pursuit thereof had consumed a large portion of my mental capacity since adolescence. Hard because as a man, promiscuity was a decorated character trait and highly accepted among American society. Hard because, at the end of the day, there was a part of me that really did want to have sex. Quite honestly, I did not know how to function without the pursuit of sex as an objective in my life. By most conventional standards, I was never "out there" or "wild" as they would say, but nonetheless my motivations and intentions were no different than the men who fell into this promiscuous category. I, too, had become overly obsessed with the physical characteristics of a woman and as a result, I found myself in a perpetual state of spiritually inconsistent behavior. So much so, that it became challenging to build anything of significance with a woman for much of my early young adult life. Not surprisingly, in the midst of this harsh reality, I could not (or would not) accept that I was being convicted to change. There were many times that I wondered if my boys experienced similar convictions. To investigate my inquiries, I would coyly bring them up in conversation, but my hopes

> *...I found myself in a perpetual state of spiritually inconsistent behavior.*

were never affirmed. In fact, my boys seemed to be ok with the fact that sex would be the "one" sin that God would deal with them on. Oh how I wished that I could have found tranquility in that bit of theological banter, but it was not that easy for me. God was not letting this sin slide with me and through a series of events, He began to draw me closer and closer to Him over the years until he had me right where He wanted - humbled and willing to listen.

For the next few months I continued to try to wrestle with God on sexual purity, but, by the Holy Spirit's interceding, did not do anything to the contrary of what He wanted from me. As a New Year's resolution of sorts, I finally repented and handed over my sin of sexual immorality to God in January 2007 once and for all. I handed it over with an understanding and expectation that God had something better for my life. I handed it over knowing that only His grace and mercy could wipe my slate clean and provide me with a fresh start. I handed it over with an understanding that I had much to learn about what it meant to walk in purity and welcomed His process of restoration. I handed it over finally, for the first time in my adult life, in a sincere attempt to be obedient to what God was asking of me. From that point forward, my life began an about-face that ultimately landed me here, in this chair, writing this book. If you would have asked me 8 years ago, as I prepared to finish up my last semester in college, would I be writing a book on sexual sin, I would have looked at you in bewilderment and chuckled to myself. But, over the years I've grown accustomed to God's sense of humor and so, here I sit, writing the book I never thought I would write, to a reader that I question if at all exists. Nevertheless, let me take you back to where it all began.

1
THE "FIRST TIME"

Psalms 51:5 – "Surely I was sinful at birth, sinful from the time my mother conceived me."

"*I*n the name of the Father, in the name of the Son, in the name of the Holy Ghost," the pastor said in that all too familiar harmonic southern Baptist tone, often called "whooping" in pastoral circles. And with that, I was quickly submerged into the water with a towel over my face and within a moment's time, lifted back up out of the water. As they dried water from my eyes, I regained consciousness to the sound of clapping and cheering. I glanced over at my parents and saw them smiling and gave them a zestful thumbs up. It was sometime in the fall of 1987, I was 6 years old and I had just been baptized. My baptism served as an exhibition for my church congregation of what had already occurred within some weeks before, when I walked down the aisle and proclaimed that I believed that Jesus Christ was the Son of God and that He was my Lord and Savior. It was now known to the world that I was a born again Christian and my life from that day forward would never be the same.

I remember it like it was yesterday and the bewilderment I had shortly after the baptism ceremony, because no supernatural activity occurred. I knew I loved Jesus and I fully accepted that He died on the cross for my sins, but I also expected my baptism to mimic the biblical stories of Pentecost in my own childish ignorance. To my surprise, no cataclysmic events occurred that day or any other day soon after for that matter, and as a result, I was a little disappointed. So, I went on with my life as any other kid would, by preoccupying myself with video games, sports and hanging with friends. However, consistent with my upbringing to that point, my parents continued to make sure that Sundays were reserved for the Lord and as such, we attended church every week. This routine would continue until I grew old enough to drive myself, during which time, church had unfortunately become relegated to an action item on my list of to-do's on Sundays. I would often find myself fully distracted during service awaiting the benediction so that I could leave and tend to whatever I had left unattended while in church. A paused video game, a phone conversation with a girl or even a favorite TV show, the substance of the matter did not matter as much as the fact that in my immaturity I had something to do. Around the same time, like most teenagers, I began to press up against my parents' rules and question everything they said. In the same token, I began to question much of what the Bible had to say about Christian living, especially those that prohibited many of the activities that I found enjoyable. I wanted to do what I wanted to do and anything or anyone that posed a threat to this goal was, in effect, my adversary and did not have my best interest at heart. Not surprisingly, one of the sins that I struggled most with to comprehend, embrace and assign contextual legitimacy to was that of sex, or as the Bible calls it, fornication. While it may have taken me a while to figure out the full extent of what fornication meant, my hormones quickly drove me to a point of decision.

> *In the same token, I began to question much of what the Bible had to say about Christian living, especially those that prohibited many of the activities that I found enjoyable.*

Her name was Leann. She was a virgin and I was not or so I told her. It is true. I told her a lie from the very beginning regarding my sexual history. From my perspective it was a "little white lie," one that could easily be addressed at a later time. But, conveniently, that time was not now. See, the timing of such an admission was critical because her willingness to allow me to take her virginity was hinged upon the security of knowing that I had the requisite experience. As such, I was forced to play this little white lie all the way out until the goal was achieved.

My relationship with Leann had really blossomed over the few months since we began dating. She had become my first real girlfriend. It was a very exciting time for me, for I thought she was "fine" and as a result, arrogantly walked around town with her in arm to ensure that everyone from my high school had a chance to see what I had locked down. Ironically, though I haughtily walked around as if I had achieved some noble feat in gaming her up, it was probably more her doing than mine; she sent the signals and I awkwardly responded as if they were my own ideas. See, Leann and I had known of each other for awhile, however, it wasn't until a house party earlier that spring that we really crossed paths and had a chance to speak to one another. Though it was a chance encounter in some ways, I knew after seeing her that night that I had to find out more about her. And so, my best friend and I did a little research and somehow, I got her phone number and gave her a call. To my disappointment, she was not in when I made that first fateful call and thus, I had to leave a message with her mother. I have to admit, I was a bit concerned that she wouldn't call back, however, my worries were relieved when she paged me (didn't everyone have a pager in the late 90's?) once she got back home that evening. When I finally mustered up the courage to call her back, we ended up talking for hours and pretty much, from that day forward, we were inseparable. The weeks to follow were filled with five and six hour long phone conversations, movie nights at one another's houses and going out to eat on dates from time to time (I was pretty cheap so these were done sparingly). Before long, we had become your quintessential high school couple. The one everyone knew and ultimately, expected to get married shortly after graduation and start a family.

Not surprisingly, Leann was the first girl that I said 'I love you' to and actually felt that I meant it. Whether I did or not could easily be debated, but nonetheless, in my mind, I felt different about her than any girl before. This difference caused me to smile when I heard her voice, to feel that tingling on the inside when she'd run her hands through my hair or to dream about her at night. And it wasn't just me that felt this. Leann did as well and as a result, she was experiencing similar manifestations of this difference herself. In response, we came to the mutual conclusion that it was time to take our relationship to the next level. Though the foreplay was fun and exciting, it had worn its welcome for two hormone-raged teenagers and as a consequence, we believed wholeheartedly that the next most logical step of our relationship would be to have sex as a testament of our devotion to one another. And so, we lustfully trudged forward, two seventeen year old virgins, with a master plan in hand.

It was one muggy afternoon in early June of 1999 when it actually happened, some three or four weeks after our verbal agreement. In all honesty, the opportunity had presented itself before, but I was too scared to go through with it. Maybe it was my pastor's voice echoing in my subconscious mind that God's will for my life was that I wait until I was married. Maybe it was my fear of not being "good" for all of the various reasons and thus damaging my sexual reputation before even starting. Or maybe, just maybe, it was my fear of getting her pregnant or contracting an STI. Whatever the reason, I had made it all the way through four years of high school, two prom nights and an ever so anticlimactic graduation night without having sex, but that noble accomplishment would end on this day. Why this day in particular – no rhyme or reason other than it was long overdue.

In prior discussions, Leann told me that she wanted to lose her virginity before graduation, but my timidity delayed things such that her wish was ultimately not granted. However, on this day, about a week or two after her graduation ceremony, we were finally ready to consummate our relationship and take it to the "next level." And then, just like that, it happened - the very thing that I had been taught against, heard my friends boast about and secretly desired to experience for myself. When we were finished, there was an awkward silence in the room. In that moment of silence my elation was quickly deflated. I felt the presence of God in the room and I immediately became ashamed. It was as if He were sitting in a rocking chair looking on just as a father assessing his child's demeanor before scolding him. I was a bit scared by all of this spooky God stuff, so I decided not to share any of it with Leann for fear of not knowing what to say and appearing inexperienced. And so, I did what any gentleman would do; I gave her a hug, a gentle kiss of adoration and left her house to head back home.

As I drove home that evening, a multitude of thoughts raced through my mind as I vividly replayed the deed of the day. I questioned whether or not she enjoyed it or if I had done it right. I wondered if we would do it again. I thought about the story I would tell my boys and how I would tell it. Again, Leann did not know it, but this was my first time too, so I was a little nervous when I saw her wincing in the middle of our sexual encounter. For me, it was not all that it was cracked up to be. I mean, the ejaculation part felt really good, but everything leading up to that was somewhat less fulfilling than I had imagined. I suppose all of the rumors about and depictions of sex purported a more out of body experience. But, no matter how she or I felt about it, I quickly came to realize that what had occurred could not be undone. We had both just gained our first experience for our sexual history resume`, which had up to this point only contained our career aspirations and a few internships.

Later that evening, Leann called and seemed pretty cheery on the other end of the receiver, which was a relief to me. Much of the ensuing conversation consisted of our typical teenage banter; however, there was a general awkwardness about the flow of the conversation. While we did not try to avoid the fact that we had done "it," we did not exactly address it head-on, either. ("It" was what we affectionately called sex in some sophomoric attempt to relegate the act itself.) I think we were both nervous and as a result, subtly danced around it. In some respects, it would make sense for Leann to have been nervous because it could be considered somewhat crass for her to have been pushing the issue. At the same time, I did not know what I was doing in the first place, so I was not really in the position to add any value to such a discussion either. Nevertheless, after a few minutes of talking, somehow or another we awkwardly backed our way into a discussion about whether or not we would do "it" again. Though I can't recall who brought it up, we eventually came to the mutual decision that we would do "it" the next time we saw each other.

And as we became more and more experiences, I began to notice that the guilt and spiritual turmoil surroinding the act of sex itself had become less and less prevalent.

As planned, the next day we zestfully met up again to once more use our bodies outside of the God-given context.

For the next three months, Leann and I would continue this pattern of sexual behavior, so much so that we had become pretty good at it; at least in our own minds. And as we became more and more experienced, I began to notice that the guilt and spiritual turmoil surrounding the act of sex itself had become less and less prevalent. Frankly, by the time the end of the summer had arrived, I felt little conviction about having sex with Leann and did not feel the presence of God bothering me anymore. I had finally achieved the freedom that I had so longed for – to enjoy the pleasure of sex without oppression; and it felt great!

Rededication

2
COLLEGE DAYS

Romans 7:19 – "For what I do is not the good I want to do; no, the evil I do not want to do – this I keep doing."

The day had finally come. I had reached young adult utopia and I was about to embark upon the "college days." My parents were rather stoic as we packed up the car and prepared to head north towards Washington, DC. I suppose the thought of their only child moving some 1200 miles away had finally begun to set in. For me, this moment in time was one filled with mixed emotions. I was sad because I'd be leaving Leann behind (she would be attending a school close to home that fall), but at the same time happy because I'd be on my own for the first time of my life. Also, I was nervous because living in DC would be nothing like that of Huntsville, AL. What about my friends? All of my boys were either staying in Huntsville or going to colleges in other parts of the South. As a result, I expected that making friends in college would be somewhat challenging. With all of these thoughts running through my head, the car finally backed out of the garage and into the street that morning. The sun had not yet broken and we were finally on our way. As we moved along down the street, I kept my eyes focused on our house, the place where I had grown from a child to a young man. Second by second, we moved further and further away until finally the house was out of view. At that moment, I felt something damp run down my face. Overwhelmed by the emotions of the moment, I let an involuntary tear escape from within. Luckily for me, it was still dark and my parent's attention was focused on the road and so, I threw a pillow on top of my head and fell asleep.

When we finally arrived on Howard University's campus on that hot and steamy day in August of 1999, the place was buzzing with activity. Freshman from all over the country and world were moving in and getting settled. We arrived fairly early and as a result, I was able to get my keys pretty quickly and check into my room with minimal hassle. After we unloaded the car, my mom took to making my bed and performing the detoxification that the room required while my dad and I worked to move furniture around and unpack luggage. After about an hour or so, we completed these activities and sat there in the room with the door open just taking it all in. On both sides of my single occupancy room there were two other freshmen partaking in the very same adventure with their relatives. As we "people watched" and conversed amongst ourselves, the time had eventually come for my parents to leave. Unlike a lot of parents that weekend, mine had no intention of hanging around for the orientation activities and thus, they were ready to make the trek back to Huntsville, Alabama the next morning. So, we headed downstairs to the lobby and out the door into the dormitory courtyard for our final farewell. As we reached the car, my dad extended his hand for a shake and I obliged. Holding each other's hand, we embraced and he told me that he was proud of me. I turned from him and leaned in towards my mom and gave her a hug and kiss on the cheek and told her thanks for all of her help. We exchanged "I love you's" and within a few minutes they were gone. As I casually walked back into the dormitory and up the steps towards my room, it began to truly sink in that I was finally on my own. No more "house" rules. In fact, I'd be able to make up my own. With this new sense of freedom, I became more and more excited about what my first semester in college would have to offer.

It is a fact that by the time I reached Howard's campus, I did not have much sexual experience at all. Sure, Leann and I had spent nearly four months perfecting our craft, but aside from her I had never been with anyone else and I must admit that this reality had me a bit apprehensive about pursuing additional notches to add to my proverbial belt. However, I figured I'd be able to buy myself some time by embracing my relationship with Leann under the auspices of faithfulness. If questioned on my seemingly lack of appetite to pursue women on campus, this would be the story that I would share and it would be sure to garner respect and alleviate any suspicion(s) surrounding my sexual vigor. But, this was just my first day and I'd have plenty of time to scheme and plot, so I got dressed and headed to the yard for the orientation activities.

It did not take very long to become acclimated to my surroundings. However, being a southern boy from Alabama with a thick accent did not serve me well as I sought out to make new acquaintances. Southern staples and phraseology such as "fixin" and "finna" were often received with mixed countenance. More specifically, I found meeting females particularly interesting as they received my southern diction as both cute and peculiar. And while these responses were ok and gave me hope that my future pursuits would not be in vain, I quickly came to realize that all of the "cool kids" were from New York or New Jersey and if you didn't say "yo" or "son" a lot, you were at the bottom of the pack of this herd.

Over the course of the next few months, I began to hang out with three guys from Chicago, William (aka Will), James and Lovell, that lived on the same floor as me. To my surprise, we became very close in a short period of time (I suppose no air condition or cable television in our dormitory may have contributed to our familial bond). They became my crew. Aside from being practically inseparable on campus, we'd spend countless hours after our club excursions analyzing the play by play and fantasizing about the women we had (and had not) danced with on any given night. In fact, these conversations oftentimes extended beyond our circle and became inclusive of the whole dormitory if a party was particularly eventful. And each crew would relish in its own stories and seek to outdo the others through some form of dramatization or reenactment of how it all went down. I found these sessions particularly humorous and looked forward to them each weekend we all went out. After the hoopla would die down, each crew would escape back into their own living quarters and a more in depth discussion would proceed, usually ending with some sort of action items/dare, getting a phone number for example, for someone to tackle the next week on campus. While getting a phone number seems innocent enough and typical of boyish fervor, the intentions behind its pursuit were never more complicated. Sex was always the end goal.

In our briefing sessions after our club rendezvous, over time we had gotten pretty comfortable sharing our own sexual experiences with one another. So much so, that just discussing who you danced with became a bore unless you were able to convey how that action translated or would translate into some future perverse action. Follow-up was everything and in the fail circumstance where no further action occurred, it was deemed coincidental, not premeditated. Each week, the stories about the club experience itself would be less and less, and the conversation would quickly shift to who "perved" who (Perv, or short for pervert, was a term we used to mean "everything, but sex"). As the conversations transitioned, I began to feel more and more uncomfortable being apart of them. Uncomfortable because I knew I would soon run out of "passes" or opportunities to come up nil and my favor with the fellas would soon fail. Shamefully, I wanted to be part of the crew and though no one said it, I knew that if I didn't eventually have a story or two to bring to the table myself, I'd be exiled. As a result of this acute understanding of the situation at hand, I decided to adopt and embrace that old tried and true philosophy of mankind - "when in Rome, do as the Romans do."

Eventually people got used to my southern drawl, and I was no longer the butt of the same old tired jokes. Things were going really well and over the course of that first semester, I met a ton of people from across the entire African Diaspora. As I met new friends and became exposed to new cultures, ideologies and environments, my character and perspective began to be impacted significantly. It was as if my consciousness had been awoken in those nascent moments on Howard's campus and it was a refreshing feeling. For the first time since leaving my parent's nest, I finally felt that I was coming into my own. But, as much as I enjoyed this renaissance moment of sorts, all of this newness and self-awareness began to create some friction between Leann and I.

Yes, Leann and I were still together after those first few months in college. However, she was still in Alabama, attending a local state university and this reality transformed our relationship into a long distance one. Quite honestly, the distance made things difficult for us because for those three or four months before college, we were around each other every day and then all of a sudden, at the snap of a finger, we were more than a thousand miles away. Since cell phone proliferation had yet to occur, we were forced to utilize phone cards to speak to each other on a daily basis. And although we had pretty constant communication, sometimes three or five hours at a time, it did not take long before the tensions grew and we began bickering over little things that at the time appeared monumental. In the thick of it, I would take the default position and attribute our arguments to Leann and her bipolar feministic mood swings. But now as I reflect on it, it was easily my immaturity that served as the primary catalyst for our contention. With tensions growing, distance setting in and my personal concession to "do as the Romans do," it was easy to see that the integrity of our relationship had become weakened and we would not last much longer. Yes, I loved Leann (or so I thought at the time), but I was only 18 years old and did not have a clue what or who I wanted out of life. Not that my indecisiveness serves as a valid argument to straining the emotional fiber of our relationship, but it was one that I could live with. After all, Howard had provided me with a fertile ground to define myself and come into my own.

By Christmas break of 1999, Leann and I had called it off. It was not a difficult break-up, but more an acquiescence of an evident reality. There was a part of me that was disappointed, but another part of me that was oddly excited because I felt that without Leann in my life I could truly enjoy the splendors that Washington, DC had to offer. Sure, there were tourist sites and all in the District, but the splendors that I was more set on exploring were those of the seven to one female to male ratio on Howard's campus at the time. I was still young and had read it say somewhere that as a "rites of passage" for manhood, every young man must at some point soil his royal oats. So, there I stood, at the conclusion of Christmas break, in the Huntsville International Airport, awaiting my call for boarding for the Northwest Airlines flight en route to Washington, DC. Though a familiar scene, this time I would be boarding the flight with a different agenda in mind and a newfound freedom that would allow me to more intimately embrace college life; finally enabled to script some stories of my own to share with the crew.

> *I was still young and had read it say somewhere that as a "rites of passage" for manhood, every young man must at some point soil his royal oats.*

No sooner than my flight touched down at Reagan International was Leann an afterthought. Like a convict out on parole, I hastily began to plot and scheme on the women I would target as my first collegiate sexual partners. To be fair, I had some feelings towards the women I identified – either physical, mental or a combination of the two. So, it was not just the sex that I was interested in, although it did serve as the precursor to any initial interest. However, it was not until I became a member of a popular campus organization in that spring semester that my plan began to see the light of day and I knew eventually it would yield a harvest.

The organization I joined was called Campus Friends. It was an organization built to support the high school to college transition for incoming freshman and ensure that their first week on campus would be a memorable one. It was a high energy, fun-loving organization and as a result, there were many people on campus, namely underclassmen, who desired to be a part of it. Unfortunately, only a select few were chosen each year. Consequently, those who were selected were introduced to the campus, with much fanfare, as individuals who possessed some special quality/characteristic that gave them an edge over the unlucky number of individuals who were not (whether true or not is debatable). As a result, once you became a member, everyone on campus knew who you were and almost instantly, you were popular.

One pink elephant in the room that often stigmatized Campus Friends was the fact that it had a history of incestuous behavior or "inbreeding" so to speak. Sure, very rarely was anyone in the organization actually related, but it was considered somewhat of a colloquial family. Because we would spend countless hours together in preparation for freshman orientation week, mutual attractions would build and usually one or two couples would emerge, while other more scandalous behavior would remain covert and beneath the surface. While this was an accepted practice amongst the Friend ranks, it was much to the chagrin of the administrative staff.

As a Campus Friend, there was a certain amount of power that one attained. This power was a direct result of the way in which the organization was portrayed to the freshman class each fall. We were the sole owners of their orientation and transition to Howard. Because of this, they looked up to us and as they matriculated, the adoration would grow. Before long, the adoration would morph into fascination, and as a Friend, you could pretty much get whatever you wanted from them. Sure, this was not all the time or with everybody, but it held true in enough instances to be valid.

Becoming a Campus Friend provided me with a gateway to exploit my longstanding master plan. The exposure, incestuous behavior and power all coalesced to create a violent cocktail which, when served chilled to someone, would cause almost instant intoxication. Unfortunately, that someone this time around was me. Not only did I gulp the cocktail as if I had previously built up the tolerance required to hold it down, but I also quickly developed a hearty appetite for it. This appetite was well suited for my newly obtained freedom and I eagerly awaited the opportunity for the two to meet head-on when I returned to school the next fall for my first orientation week. Until then, I had to wait because by the time I became a member of the organization, the spring semester was almost over.

Aside from my affiliation with the Campus Friends, I had begun to see glimmers of what the college experience could offer sexually that spring semester. I experienced quite a few "pervs" and had some rather close calls, so from my view of the world at the time, things were for the most part on the up and up. With these fresh experiences in hand and my new organizational affiliation, sophomore year had all the ingredients and potential to be an interesting year. But, before I could get there, I had the summer ahead of me to get some much needed practice.

Summers were usually uneventful for me, but I was determined to make a story out of this one. After all, I was back in Huntsville with a newfound sense of self from the prior year's matriculation and had home-court advantage which put the odds heavily in my favor. At home, there was a lot of unfinished business with females from my past. Remember, Leann was the only person that I had had sex with in Alabama (or anywhere else for that matter) and because I seemed to have blossomed so late, I felt it necessary to seek closure with some of the women I dated back in high school. But, the monkey wrench in my plan was that Leann was back home for the summer too and though we had broken up during the previous Christmas, we had remained friends and in contact for much of the spring semester. As a result, this timid communication pattern made for an awkward situation when I returned home, as our status hung in the air. Nevertheless, Leann would eventually become just another woman that summer. One with a higher priority, but part of a growing team of women nonetheless. And so, I marched onward toward my goal of creating an artistically perverse narrative.

While the majority of that summer at home yielded few "new" results (Leann and I would find ourselves in the throes of lust a time or two during the summer), there were two unsuspecting women with whom I created relationships with and subsequently, sex ensued. The first woman was much older than me and I think the sheer joy of saying I had sex with an older woman was the primary catalyst for the action more so than being enamored by any physical/mental characteristics. In fact, the first time we got together that summer I perved and then, in our next rendezvous, I closed the deal. After that, we didn't have much further interaction. While at first this might seem crass, she admitted to me that she suffered from nymphomania and as a result, she required nothing of me other than my God-given appendage. Thus, she had gotten what she wanted and I had achieved what I aspired to do and as a result, I quickly cut her off in order to free myself up for the next opportunity.

The second woman was a friend from the past who I had always considered cute, but never much more than that. For the remainder of that summer my time was spent with her as we pursued an open-ended relationship with no real long-term goals attached. For all intents and purposes, she was my girlfriend that summer. It was supposed to be a refreshing change for me to be in a pseudo relationship with no commitment – every man's dream I had heard; the antithesis of my relationship with Leann. But, in this situation, it did not seem as glamorous and it actually caused me to second guess myself. I found the foreplay enjoyable, but as we finally climbed into bed and completed our way around third base with a slide into home plate, the excitement and fulfillment that had previously accompanied a new experience was absent. In fact, instead of jubilation, I was overcome by a very sobering mood. I felt empty. This feeling was foreign to me and I was completely perplexed as to its origins. What was the issue?

At the time, I attributed it to the fact that she was not Leann and that I had actually made a mistake in breaking up with her the past semester. However, as I reflect back on this experience, it is clear that the real root of this void was that in my expression of freedom that summer, I had begun to further distance myself from God. The void I felt, therefore, was the result of a vacancy left behind. No way was I able or ready, at the time, to acknowledge that this feeling had anything to do with God. So, I continued on as a mindless soldier carrying out a fruitless mission for the remainder of the summer until I returned back to campus in preparation for freshman orientation week.

> *I had begun to further distance myself from God. The void I felt, therefore, was the result of a vacancy left behind.*

In my feeble-mindedness, I had very high expectations for my sophomore year. I really did. But, it ended up being somewhat underwhelming to say the least. Still no deals closed in college, but a ton of close calls. Time and time again, I would be either in a woman's room or my own and we would both lie naked in the bed and then something would come up that stopped the act just short of penetration. Whether it was the picture of Leann on the window sill (yes, we had gotten back together, but we would be off and on for much of the year), a guilty conscience about an estranged boyfriend back home or just plain old fear of me running my mouth; whatever the reason, I just could not seem to close the deal, ever. It became quite frustrating after awhile, especially since my boys were closing deals like Wall Street fat cats.

I can vividly remember sitting around the room with them after we got back in from the club, in similar fashion as we did our freshman year, every weekend sharing tales of what occurred the night before. As the months passed, each story became more and more perverse. As my turn would come up, my story would carry a similar theme, "I perved, but..." It became somewhat of an inside joke amongst us and they meekly attributed my misfortune to the "good guy" syndrome. You know the good guy syndrome, right? This is the syndrome that subscribes to the belief that women are more likely to have casual sex with the "bad guy," the one that they would never take home to meet the parents. As a result, if you were the type of guy that a woman would seriously consider a future with, you probably would not succeed with getting her to compromise her moral qualities (waiting for marriage) for you due to her image preservation in the face of a "good guy."

While this syndrome has been well tested, I was not willing to accept any justification for my inability to close the proverbial deal. So, I left Howard that summer, on my way to New York for an internship, with a bit of a chip on my shoulder – eager to get back to D.C. to crack the cycle of ineptness with women that had plagued me.

Perhaps, my unsuccessful track record that year was the result of God protecting me from dangers "seen and unseen." But no, that did not make sense because why would He care so much about me? I mean, I was not diligent in my studies of His Word nor was I a member of anyone's church. In fact, I don't think I knew where a church was outside of the campus Chapel. Nevertheless, the summer of 2001 had come and gone before I knew it, and the only significant thing was that Leann and I had gotten back together (again!). However, by the end of the summer, we had broken up. It was kind of the way our relationship went those days – back and forth with no real conclusion at the end. A part of me started to believe that she and I were beginning to grow apart. I don't know why we kept going back and forth with each other, but for some reason we both left the door open each time it ended. Maybe it was the fact that we were each other's "first." I had always heard people talk about the significance of one's first, but never really put too much stock into it. Maybe it was the supposed spiritual bond that is created by way of sexual intercourse. But, that did not make much sense because I didn't have a problem shutting the door on any of the other women. Whatever the reason, I wasn't going to rack my brain too long as the main point was that I'd be returning to campus as single as ever for the second time in my collegiate career. There was one key difference this time though. I would be an upperclassman and I was sure that my newfound status along the social hierarchy would carry some weight for me. Additionally, I had fraternal aspirations that year and if I hadn't closed a deal prior to that process beginning, I was confident that shortly thereafter I would succeed.

As I recall, the majority of my junior year was all but a blur, with the exception of the beginning and ending. Finally, the incestuous behavior inherent in becoming a member of Campus Friends bore fruit. No sooner than I returned to campus did she pick me out as her target. That's right. She picked me. At this point in my journey, I still subscribed to that piece of wisdom which said it was the man's role to pursue, but in this case she was quicker to her gun than I. Who was I to deny her that right? And so, over the course of those two weeks of freshman orientation preparation and events, we flirted intensely. To my pleasure, the culmination of our flirtatious behavior came to a head one evening right after school began. Now, for purposes of full disclosure, an opportunity to close the deal had presented itself before this particular night, but as in prior instances, something held me back. As a result, I made a personal pledge to myself that this time would be different. Plus, I already told my boys about the first "close call" and as a result, they had high expectations of me for this encore event and little tolerance for anything less than a closed deal. So, here we were. She and I, ready to embark on a sexual escapade. With inhibitions aside, we proceeded forward on the erotic rollercoaster, *the Fornicator*, until our adventure eventually came to a screeching halt. I was overcome by a state of euphoria when it was over because I had finally gotten over the hump. I finally had sex with someone at Howard. But, no sooner than I had gotten over my hump and began to look forward to future indiscretions, another journey began that would change the dynamic of my collegiate experience forever.

If you will recall, shortly after the beginning of my freshman year I joined Campus Friends in part to establish myself on campus and increase my own popularity. And yes, I am quite aware of the vain nature of these objectives, however, I dare to say that my ambitions and associated motivations were any different than others who roamed the campus during that same time period. Well, now I was a junior and felt that I had achieved much success.I had gained a fairly decent reputation on campus, but there was still more room for my ego to grow. See, I grew up with black greek letter organization (BGLO) influence all around me as my father was a member of Kappa Alpha Psi, Fraternity, Inc. So, it was not a surprise that by the time I had become acclimated to collegiate life, I would soon find myself inquiring about such organizations. During my inquisitions, I learned that the fraternity of my father's choosing was not on campus due to a suspension. This was somewhat disappointing as I had always dreamed of being able to do the secret shakes and share other ritualistic behaviors with him, but I was also well aware of the fact that a decision to join any organization would ultimately lie with me. As such, I continued my search into these organizations and found myself impressed with the young men of Alpha Phi Alpha, Fraternity, Inc.

It is probably debatable which organization was most popular at the time, but to me the Alpha's carried themselves in a manner that really distinguished them from the pact and furthermore, seemed to best reflect the type of man I was looking to become. For all the noble reasons related to the upliftment of African-American community at large, there were infinitely as many selfish motives that lied beneath my motives to seek membership with them. And so it went, from the fall of 2001 through and into the spring of 2002, I traveled the street paved with black and old gold toward Alphaland...

On March 29, 2002 it was a beautiful bright and sunny day. The weatherman had called for rain with an occasional thunderstorm, but we were spared because by the time the clock tower's bell rang, the birds were in full flight above us and there was not a cloud in sight. It was the day all nine of us had long awaited for. It was our probate day (the day when we would be officially introduced to the campus as members of Alpha Phi Alpha) and there was nothing that could crush the immense pride that we had. After we had finished getting dressed for the occasion, painted each other's faces, said a prayer and took a shot of Wild Turkey whiskey, we were ready to exit the Chemistry building in the lower quadrangle and head up the steep stairway to be reintroduced to the Mecca, Howard University. As we each took our turns running up the stairwell, the adrenaline began to run rapidly through my veins and before I knew it, it was my turn. To my delight, when I reached the top and perused the landscape, it seemed like there were a thousand students outside waiting for our unveiling. Although tradition held that no one should know that you were on "line" in advance of the probate, the word had leaked by this time and as a result, all of our friends and family were well prepared with pomp and circumstance to cheer us on.

"Line!" our dean said emphatically.

"Dean, yes, dean!" we responded in unison to the roar of the crowd.

"Y'all, ready?" he blurted out rhetorically.

"Dean, yes, dean!" we shouted back at the top of our lungs.

Stomp. Stomp. Stomp. Stomp. "We are...the Sphinxmen and we're...moving up slowly..." Stomping as hard as we could, marching in unison, we pressed forward singing the songs of the fraternity with our soon-to-be brothers guiding us every step of the way.

The probate lasted about three hours and no sooner than it ended, did we begin promoting our probate after-party at the club that evening. I was ecstatic over this new accomplishment. I was now a member of Alpha Phi Alpha, Fraternity, Inc., Beta Chapter. I had officially sealed my place in Howard and Alpha's history. I remember thinking to myself that day how my legacy had begun its script – chapter 1. I guess my excitement was warranted by the amount of sacrifice I made to complete the process and obtain membership. But, somewhere along the way – maybe the months leading up to that probate day or maybe it occurred during the probate show as I admired the gawking of the other students looking on, specifically the women – I seemed to have lost a part of myself.

To be fair, the journey made me a better man in many respects. For example, I had become more socially conscious and aware. I had been exposed to people and things that would not have been afforded to me without membership. And though all of those things were good and reason for celebration, there was a piece of me that was lost along the way as well. Somehow and somewhere along the way, my selfish motives dwarfed the more noble reasons I joined the organization and I became so self-absorbed that it would take years to undo the damage.

> Somehow and somewhere along the way, my selfish motives dwarfed the more noble reasons I joined the organization and I became so self-absorbed that it would take years to undo the damage.

I suppose the biggest driver for my newfound attitude and self-absorption could have been related to the amount of attention that we received post probate. But then, that would place the blame on others instead of me. Now, as I look back at the situation, I realize that the root cause can best be traced to my own relentless pursuit of status. I had always been a very driven person and becoming an Alpha only fed what was becoming a monster of an ego. In the game of life, I had not "lost" very many games dating back as far as I could remember. I had been immensely blessed and reached a point where I began to credit my success to my own efforts. And unfortunately, being one of the select few (nine in total) to actually make it through the "Alpha" journey only exacerbated this belief. I quickly developed a smug disposition towards those young men who either chose that it was not for them after a failed attempt and also towards those who never attempted. To make matters worse, my mere membership granted me a superfluous campus status, and further fed my ego. Bathed in conceit, I re-emerged on campus as an emboldened caricature of myself and like a lion in the jungle, passionately sought out female prey to pounce upon – I wanted to be the Alpha male.

To this day, my line brothers are some of the coolest brothers I know. All of them are very intelligent, ambitious and handsome. This fact made it extremely difficult for me to be content with myself during those days following our initiation into the fraternity. Whether they excelled inside or outside the classroom, the one common denominator between them all, with the exception of maybe one, was that sex with women was as normal for them as brushing one's teeth in the morning. In fact, many of them had sex with new women the very same day we crossed (i.e. one night stands) and others shortly thereafter. And though I had finally overcome my hurdle of sex on campus prior to my journey towards becoming a member, I was still heavily burdened by the fact that I had only had sex with one woman on campus. This reality provided ample material and oftentimes landed me right at the butt of the jokes from my line brothers. Not that they had malicious intent, but there was a bit of a competitive spirit (and peer pressure to the utmost) in it all and they were amused that even with my newly obtained status, my sexual reality had not changed much. But, these jokes did not last too long as within a few weeks or so of crossing I had finally found another victim to satiate my sexual curiosity.

Ironically, she told me that she was a virgin. I do not imagine that I took her to be lying at the time, but I was perplexed by the fact that she would allow me to be her first. See, Sidney and I had been dealing with each other for much of the time that I was on "line," going through the process to become a member of Alpha Phi Alpha. There were countless instances during that time period where I tried to have sex with her, but to no avail. So, as one could imagine, on this particular night I could not believe that she was going to actually going to let me do it.

She arrived at my room late in the evening as standard per our "arrangement" (we usually "hooked up" after we got back in from the club). After a few moments of conversation, we eventually found ourselves in a familiar position; lying in the bed side by side. And though the scene was familiar, I, under the influence of male bravado, still held some optimism that the results of this night would be different. *Well, here goes.* As I reached for a condom, she laid there looking a bit nervous and so, I checked to see if she was sure that this was what she wanted to do and she obliged. I continued on my mission and in less than five minutes it was over – yeah, just like that. *Oops*. I slowly and cautiously looked up at her in order to assess fulfillment, but she did not have any true expression of disappointment, as this was her first time and I suppose she had no real expectations. Though I was embarrassed about the duration, I was relieved that she didn't have the sexual history to evaluate the evening's performance. Or so I thought. Maybe it was nervous energy, but whatever it was I had failed to perform and my self confidence was completely shot. With my limited sexual resume on campus, I was extremely concerned that performances like these would surely inhibit me from landing any future deals if word ever got out.

The experience with Sidney was not one of my prouder moments in that spring of 2002, but it was part of the reality of sex. Sometimes it would be good and sometimes it would not be good, and the not so good times I always preferred remained between me and the other person. While I was eventually able to move on from this instance, it definitely stifled my sexual appetite a bit for a few months. So much so, that I became a bit "gun shy" following that incident. Interestingly enough, after the sexual encounter with Sidney, she began to act differently (in my opinion). Although we had been dealing with each other for quite some time, we had never gone on an official date outside of our dorm rooms. So, a few days after we had sex, Sidney asked me to go to the movies with her. Now, in normal circumstances, this request would not have been so odd, but given our history I found it a bit peculiar. I am not sure exactly how I got out of it, but I am sure I conjured up some lame excuse. Whatever the excuse was, it obviously was not the least bit legitimate because a few days later, Sidney again asked to go on a date. At this point I was annoyed and rudely told her to chill out with all the seriousness. I inquired about why she was acting weird and told her to give me some space. I can vividly remember the look on her face; a look of both disappointment and anger. See, Sidney had been there for me when I needed her during the period I was on "line." But, with all of the options available to me now that I was an Alpha, I had quickly forgotten how much she had done for me. Sadly, I do not think I cared much either, especially given the fact that I had had sex with her already. Truth be told, I was not interested in a relationship or anything that resembled one at the time. My main objective was to increase my numbers to remain relevant amongst my line brothers – an objective that would become fully vested by the middle of my senior year.

By the second semester of my senior year I had finally hit my stride – better late than never, right? Meeting women and closing the deal with them was not as much of a task anymore. I was keeping a fairly good pace with my line brothers and we had all fully realized the benefits of becoming members of a fraternity on a college campus. Women came and women went as the year progressed. Whether I met them through sister organizations, the classroom or walking around campus, it seemed as if I pretty much had my choice of women. By the time graduation had arrived, I had amassed a fairly respectable number count by male standards and felt that I had finally achieved manhood. As shallow as that may sound, I felt that life really could not get any better. In fact, the very morning of my graduation ceremony, I remember looking over in my bed at the woman accompanying me that evening and saying to myself that I would truly miss those days. As I laid there and recounted the prior night's events, she awoke abruptly in an inebriated slumber and began to gather her stuff to head to her room. Her family was waiting to meet her for the commencement exercises to begin in just a few hours. Before she left, she leaned in and gave me a kiss that both represented affection, but also symbolized the end of a chapter in both of our lives. As the door shut behind her, I rolled onto my back, let out a sigh and looked towards the ceiling clutching my head as it throbbed violently from the celebratory libations the night before. I thought to myself that my collegiate experience had been a good run after all.

While I had somewhat of a slow start, in the end I achieved a considerable amount. However, as I relished in recanting the years' sexual indiscretions, I noticed that that old familiar awkward emptiness inside had returned. As these thoughts raced through my mind, my eyelids shut and my subconscious mind began to fixate on a figure that appeared to be shaping itself right before me. It took a second, but it was not long before I could make out what it was. It was a familiar face; one that I had been running from the entire time while I was in college. There He was again, just like He had been in earlier times in my life, looking down on me in disappointment. I am not sure if the disappointment this time was related to the very act that had just been committed or an aggregate of what had become of my collegiate experience. Whatever it was, I felt convicted and ashamed to some degree, but I could not let that bother me – after all it was my graduation day and that meant it was time to celebrate!

3
WELCOME TO
THE REAL WORLD

1 John 2:16 – "For everything in the world – the cravings of sinful man, the lust of his eyes and the boasting of what he has and does – comes not from the Father but from the world."

*F*rom my perspective, I was your ordinary college graduate. Proudly, I had gone through four years of rigorous coursework, organizational inductions, and fraternal exploitations and somehow obtained a bachelors degree in chemical engineering with honors. It was unbeknownst to me how this achievement was possible, other than the possibility that someone or "someones" were praying for me each and every night. Good thing they were, because my personal prayer life was pretty abysmal during the majority of my four years in college. The fail instances where it did emerge, I managed to relegate it to a life triaging practice more than religious duty. As with my prayer life, so went my church participation

...my personal prayer life was pretty abysmal during the majority of my four years in college. The fail instances where it did emerge, I managed to relegate it to a life triaging practice more than religious duty.

and/or affiliation. I could probably count on two hands the number of times I went to church while in school. Sure, there are many hokey theological mantras that I could provide to justify why this behavior was not at all a negative thing, but the truth is that I would be denying the truth inside. In fact, some who bore witness during my matriculation chose to diagnose my actions as an occurrence of rebellious upheaval that every young adult must go through. Thank God for these scholars because they provided me with a shelter in which I could enjoy refuge. So, it's no wonder I felt no guilt as I received my degree knowing that if it had not been for the Lord on my side, it would not have been possible. And so I went, across the stage as proud as ever that my collegiate journey had finally concluded. To top that off, I had already accepted a job and was well on my way to being dubbed a success by family and peers. Not that this designation was validated, but as a culture that is still in its nascent stages of generations without overt oppression, it was customary to herald any black man who received a degree from an accredited university and cater to his every need until he decided to remove the pacifier himself.

My days at Howard University were enjoyable and I find it amazing that I was able, in all my sin, to exit physically unscathed. However, there were a few scares here or there; times when I went to the clinic to get a check-up in response to what I perceived to be an irregular feeling "down there."

The reality is, and always will be, that there are consequences related to sex. While condoms have a fairly high degree of success in protecting the physical consequences, they still aren't 100% effective. And it is this margin of error that kept me awake many nights as I wondered to myself if I had gotten a girl pregnant or if I had contracted something. Going to the clinic to get checked for STI's had to be the most uncomfortable and embarrassing experience ever. In the age of modern medicine, there's no reason for them to still need the infamous "Q-tip" anymore, but I guess they have kept it around as a preventative measure; the discomfort it causes does make you rethink your actions. Nonetheless, as I would sit there with the nurse preparing for Q-tip insertion and blood to be drawn, my mind would begin racing nervously in anticipation of the results. However, no matter how much I anticipated or how fast my mind raced, it would be a few days before I would find out the true verdict.

The period of time between getting tested and finding out my results was the always the worst. It was in that time that I would replay each and every sexual encounter, by the minute, in search for any suspect action that may have made me vulnerable to disease. It was crazy because as I would search and scan my memory bank, I would be a nervous wreck even though I had always been careful per se and used condoms. The sad part of it all is that this anxiety had come upon me as a result of my own actions. I would always think to myself that maybe, just maybe it wasn't worth it. I mean, sex was good, but the idea that I could have contracted something life-threatening was a very sobering reality; one that I did not have to face until I went to get tested. And now that I was faced with it, I was destined to identify some instance that I could point the finger at as the potential culprit for my proverbial demise. Not surprisingly, it wouldn't take long before I'd find a plausible occurrence to call into question. But, identified or not, it didn't matter because what had been done had been done, and within a few days I would find out the collateral damage of my actions.

The sad part of it all is that this anxiety had come upon me as a result of my own actions.

Though I always expected the worst, I was very fortunate during my college days because each time the results would come in, they were negative. HIV? Negative. Gonorrhea? Negative. Syphilis? Negative. Genital Herpes? Negative. Chlamydia? Negative. And the list goes on...I was continually spared.

While one would expect that God's mercy in this area of my life would have been humbling, at the time it had the opposite effect on me. Unfortunately, I took it for granted and credited my negative test results to be a function of my own carefulness and attention to detail. As a result, I left college as a new and improved self; a cocky and slightly abrasive individual ready to embark on adulthood. Now, I do not note these adjectives in an attempt to highlight what I perceived as my positive qualities at the time, but more to express their relevance to my newly established character. With exuberant pride and an ego to match, I packed up my bags and moved to Lansdale, Pennsylvania to begin my career as a working professional. No more college campus, no more financial aid and no more student status as Lansdale would become my new home; a place where my road into the real world would begin.

That first year out of college living on my own and working my first corporate gig was interesting. Through what I deemed to be my hard core negotiation skills (God's grace), I was able to command a fairly competitive salary that afforded me a few of life's luxuries. As such, I practically ran the streets Thursday through Sunday in an attempt to recreate similar realities to those that I experienced in the District of Columbia. I wanted to be everywhere and anywhere to be part of the action. Though most of my crew went in different directions after graduation, I was fortunate enough to link up with a friend from one of my internships in the Philadelphia area when I returned. He became my partner in crime (or I his), and we made sure to make our first year out of school as memorable as possible. And speaking of being everywhere and anywhere, creating memorable experiences, did I mention my girlfriend yet?

Shortly after I left Howard, I made a commitment to a young woman and we formally became boyfriend and girlfriend. Her name was Rian and I can remember the very first moment I laid eyes on her outside of Crampton Auditorium after the Mr. & Mrs. Howard University pageant in the fall of my senior year. Honestly, when I saw her standing there I was quite intimidated, but my line brother pressed me to say something and make a move or he would. So, I motioned for her to come towards me and I met her on her way. I introduced myself and we exchanged information. Fast forward 8-months or so and here we were, a "Cosby-ian" couple. I was Cliff and she was Claire. This was probably the first real relationship I had been in since Leann, and I actually found it quite refreshing. Being that we had the same southern roots and went to the same academic institution, we had a lot in common. Unfortunately though, Rian was two years younger than me and when I moved to Lansdale post graduation, she remained behind in DC. Now typically, such distance would cause significant strain on a relationship, especially one that is relatively new. However, we managed to keep things fairly stable by becoming close acquaintances with I-95 and making it a point to visit one another almost every weekend.

When I wasn't traveling back and forth from Pennsylvania to DC (visiting Rian), I was back in Lansdale hanging with the fellas and auditioning as a "rolling stone." Through the course of that first year out of college I had begun to get the swing of things on the job front and my relationship with Rian was going pretty well. To sum it up, I was making good money and had a nice-looking girlfriend. What more could I ask for? Sure, I may have lacked progression in some of the more core aspects of my life, but at a surface level I was fairly content. From the outside looking in, everything looked great! I rarely attended church, but then again I was busy running the streets and church would have only served to inhibit my ability to fully roll as a stone. Plus, there was really no rush in getting back involved in the church. After all, I was just 22 years old, so why the need to be all "churchy" at such a young age? No one likes a "super Christian" anyway do they?

Sure, I may have lacked progression in some of the more core aspects of my life, but at a surface level I was fairly content. From the outside looking in, everything looked great!

As that first year out of college came to a close, I began to notice that the emptiness inside that I had experienced in the past was back once more. It was peculiar because, as I stated earlier, I had in my possession all of the things that the world defined as valuable. Even more peculiar, this time the emptiness was not specifically tied to a sexual event as it had been in the past; it just kind of evolved on its own into a sustained emotion that would not go away. I had more friends than I could count and I was well-respected by my peers on the job. Life had dealt me a good hand and yet there was still a void. Maybe my new environment, new job and/or new girlfriend had distracted me, but it was not apparent that there was anything missing. With introspective curiosity in hand, the next couple of months would prove to be the beginning of an evolution in my life. It was in those months that I would come to find out that "what" I was looking for to fill the emptiness was actually a "who."

It all began one day in June of 2004. I had just moved to New Jersey with one of my best friends from college, Will. If you recall, Will and I had met that first day of my freshman year. Our friendship grew immensely over those collegiate years. We became even closer after we graduated as a result of our close proximity to one another (he lived in NJ and I lived in PA). As luck would have it, an opportunity arose that allowed me to move to New Jersey after my first year of working and lo and behold, we became roommates. It was sure to be a year full of young adult debauchery and irresponsibility.

At any rate, it was evening that day and the air outside was stiff and compressing. I remember leaving work a little early to head to the local grocery store to pick up some items for my date later that night. Honestly, there was no emotion better than leaving work on a Friday with a date on the horizon. There was just something about it that made me feel achieved. Now, I'd love to embellish and tell of how these dates were with various women across the country, but the reality is not as entertaining. Most times, these Friday night rendezvous consisted of Rian and I connecting and going out to eat or to catch a movie. However, as a result of some trite argument a few months prior that I cannot recall, Rian and I were going through one of our rockier patches. As such, I was preparing for a visit from an old college buddy of mine. She and I had gone back and forth performing the relationship tango in our college days, but never quite became an item. Although I'm not quite sure why we never became an official entity, the curiosity of what could have been remained for some time after graduation. And this particular weekend, I intended to explore that option.

When I arrived at the grocery store, a stench of stale corrugated boxes and seafood filled the air. As I proceeded through the store to the wine aisle, I noticed a shelf containing Rick Warren's *Purpose Driven Life* among other national bestsellers. Ironically, many of my friends had been ranting and raving about this book for weeks, but I had no desire to follow the crowd and had resisted purchasing it. Now, at the time, I was still struggling with an emptiness inside and had not quite figured out how to fill it. I'd spoken to close friends and relatives about it and most would point to God and spirituality, but I wasn't quite ready to accept that reality just yet. It just seemed like a silly notion. I knew God and had been a Christian for a large part of my life. What was it about my life now that required some sort of supernatural interaction with Him? I didn't have to have it before. Nevertheless, I did find the timing of being placed in the grocery store while wrestling with this issue and running into this highly recommended book, a bit intriguing. So much so, that I received seeing the book adjacent to the wine aisle as some type of divine intervention and decided to concede and purchase it...in addition to my bottle of wine, of course. When I got home that evening I tossed the book onto the bed and prepared my abode for the company that would be arriving within the hour. I had no intention of reading the book anytime in the near future.

About a month or so passed since I purchased the book and I was becoming fairly acquainted with the New Jersey area. I found myself quite fond of a church that a co-worker had recommended. So much so, that I was attending service fairly regularly and even participated in its weekly bible study sessions. I found the messages on Sunday mornings and the discussions on Wednesday evenings very relevant. And for the first time, I had begun to develop a genuine spiritual life; one not predicated on what God could do for me, but one focused on learning about Him. It was refreshing. As I began to experience what some may call a spiritual rejuvenation, I noticed that the emptiness within began to slowly recede. One Saturday afternoon as I sat scanning my bedroom aimlessly, my eyes caught *Purpose Driven Life* sitting on the bookshelf. I reached over and grabbed it and opened it up to briefly peruse in order to see what all the hoopla was about. As I read the introduction, I was surprisingly engaged and intrigued to read more. With the prior week's sermon on my mind, a nagging emptiness within yearning to be filled and a mental acquiescence of sorts, I decided that it was finally time to go ahead and read the book. After all, what did I have to lose?

> *... I had begun to develop a genuine spiritual life; one not predicated on what God could do for me, but one focused on learning about Him.*

I've always been a pretty disciplined person. In fact, many of my friends would describe my behavior at times as "extreme" because once I made my mind up to do something, I usually pursued it with reckless abandon. I rarely took baby steps, which was oftentimes at my own detriment. I suppose the reason for this extremist "off/on," "black/white," behavior was rooted in my own impatience. Instead of being patient and allowing time to take its course, I always tried to fast forward life. And not surprisingly, I applied this same logic to the reading of *Purpose Driven Life*.

Now, if I was going to read, I was going to make sure that I fully devoted myself to it because I had reached a point in my life where I wanted God inspired answers. I searched to find the answers myself, but to no avail, I came up empty at every nook and cranny investigated. I was all out of fresh ideas on how to fill the gaping hole in me that had been a burden for months, and present for years. It was this loss of words, ideas and actions that led me to relinquish control.

Furthermore, being the carnal being that I was, I struggled to comprehend how God could forgive me for all of my transgressions.

With *Purpose Driven Life*, I saw an opportunity to restart the clock of life. Truthfully, I was ashamed to go boldly before God and query him on my emptiness. While I had started to attend a church fairly regularly at this point, I was ashamed of my past. I knew I knew better, but my actions did not at all resemble those of someone who called himself a child of God. Furthermore, being the carnal being that I was, I struggled to comprehend how God could forgive me for all of my transgressions. Steeped in guilt, I viewed *Purpose Driven*

Life as a more indirect approach to the issue. It was all that I had the courage to attempt at the time. Though indirect, I did however, commit to taking it seriously and proceeded with an intense focus.

In an effort to remove any distractions that could potentially inhibit God from speaking to me while reading, I decided to give up five of my vices, or false idols, to truly focus on the 40-day spiritual journey that Rick Warren had mapped out in his book. The five things that I gave up were sex, alcohol, clubs, R&B and Hip-Hop music and some of my favorite television shows. I chose these five things because for a large part of my life, they contributed to my prodigal ways. While sex was an obvious vice, or distraction that needed to be removed, the others were a bit more obscure. Alcohol, though I never considered myself a lush, was a tool that I used to remove my inhibitions when in pursuit of women. In my adult life, I allowed alcohol to become a prerequisite for a good time and an excuse for indiscretions. As such, I knew that I would have to let it go if I intended to hear from God. Clubs, on the other hand, were the environments fueling my sinful desires. Sure, I'd go to clubs with my boys and we'd have a genuinely good time, but there was always an ulterior motive present. Given the right opportunity to strike up a conversation with some unassuming woman, any of us would have left the so-called male bonding moment to pursue libido fulfillment.

With sex and alcohol already on the chopping block, the next logical thing to extricate was clubs, because without sex as a goal and alcohol as the catalyst, clubbing quickly became a waste of time. Lastly, R&B and Hip-Hop music and television were added to my list because I viewed these two things as negative influences. Regardless of whether or not I consciously tried to emulate what I heard in a song ("Lovers and Friends") or saw on a TV show (any multitude of sexual innuendos shown under the guise of "reality"), the fact remained that each moment I allowed the lyrics of a song or the images from a show to enter into my consciousness, I was feeding the exact being I was trying to suppress. Many would view the latter two of the five a bit extreme, but I did not let that bother me because I was acutely aware of the negative impact that they had on my life.

... each moment I allowed the lryics of a song or the images from a show to enter into my consciousness. I was feeling the exact being I was trying to suppress.

After choosing these five things, the first thing I did was email my close friends to ask for their support and accountability in the journey. Many of them were surprised, but assured me that they would be there to support me in any capacity needed. At the same time, I informed Rian. Yes, we had gotten back together and I thought of it as a good thing. We were able to reconcile our differences/issues and were back together stronger than ever.

Now, if you've done your math, she and I had been together for about a full year by now and unfortunately, one of the very things I had given up would have a direct impact on our relationship: sex. Sex was something that Rian and I shared and had shared for the majority of our relationship (even when apart). In all fairness, our relationship consisted of much more than sex. We were true companions and enjoyed the company of one another immensely. However, the reality was that this companionship was built on something that would now be removed from the equation as a result of the journey I was about to embark upon. For Rian and I, sex existed long before true companionship was born. It was there at every point from initial infatuation leading up to our subsequent relationship. Whether in physical form or my subconscious mind, by way of my fantastical desires, sex had been implicitly woven deeply into the fabric of our relationship since day one. Consequently, I knew the conversation would be challenging, but nevertheless, one that had to be had.

When I informed Rian of my decision to give up sex, alcohol, clubs, R&B and Hip-Hop music and television, she didn't seem surprised at all. She said that she understood what I was trying to accomplish and supported me. I was ecstatic. Here I thought she would be looking for a backdoor to exit the relationship, but instead she was all for it. I was so excited about the conversation that I asked her to read along with me. The idea of both of us reading a book on finding one's purpose was amazing to me and I thought to myself about the impact that it could have on our future together. To my surprise, though she tried at first, shortly after beginning the book she decided not continue, as she didn't feel the same way about it as I did. She was my girlfriend and wanted to support me, but at the same time, she couldn't force feed a "purpose journey" on herself, and she had to be honest about that. I understood and empathized with her because I myself didn't want to read it either just a short time ago. While a bit disappointed, what was most important to me was that I had her support. So, with Rian's support and accountability partners on deck, I began my 40-day journey to find my God-given purpose by way of *Purpose Driven Life*.

Over the course of the next forty days, I began to engage in deep introspection prompted by the end of chapter questions that the book laid out. I began to look at my life, where I was and what I was doing with it. I was fairly happy with where I was professionally (from a career progression standpoint), but what I found most perplexing at the time was my frustration with the work that I was doing. Honestly, I suppose my happiness had a direct correlation to the amount of compensation I received for the time I bartered. At the time, I was in my second year of my rotational program, which was considered the program for the "up and coming" professionals at my company. So in theory, I should have been content, but something about it just did not feel right. It was as if I were trying to place a square peg through a circle hole. I was not the least bit fulfilled. But, as most of us do, I ignored it and chalked it up as part of the "welcome to the real world" experience about which many elders in my life had warned me.

Before long, day 40 had come and gone and I was faced with some critical decisions to make. I was really proud that I had made it the entire 40 days without slipping on any of my commitments. So proud, that I felt invincible to the vices of the world and entitled to God's tremendous blessings on my life. After all, who else did I know that had done something like this? However, aside from what I felt I deserved as a result of my "achievement" there were still some heavy questions looming. Did I hear God speak to me? Was the purpose of the 40 day journey achieved? What do I do now that the journey is over? Do I continue the commitments or go back to my old way of life? Unfortunately, at the time, I honestly had no definitive answers to those questions. It was odd because I was unable to clearly articulate what had happened to me over that 40 day period. I felt dazed after it. Though somewhat discombobulated, one thing that was evident was the fact that I had undergone an intense mental, physical and spiritual detoxification. This purge provided me with a renewed and untainted perspective on life and what mattered most. But, I must admit, I was afraid that this renewal would only last as long as I remained isolated from others and the lifestyle that I once embraced. And no sooner than I completed the journey did I have to face that harsh reality.

> ...I must admit, I was afraid that this renewal would only last as long as I remained isolated from others and the lifestyle that I once embraced.

Rian too was very excited for me that the journey was over and that I had stuck by my guns in doing it. While excited and proud, she was, however, curious about the post-journey state of our relationship. A few days after day 40 she asked inquisitively if we were going to have sex again, since it appeared that other areas of my life were returning to a "steady-state" of sorts (Hot 97 once again blasted on my car radio. Will and I had resumed our pre-journey activities and began pounding the pavement of NYC again in search of a "good time."). Defensively, I quickly responded by adopting a victim mentality and accused her of pressuring me to have sex (oh, the irony). Truthfully, I was not the victim in this scenario, she was. I was the one who changed, not her. I imposed a new lifestyle on her and by right, she wanted clarity on what our future would look like as a result of this lifestyle change. But, at the time I was not in a place to discern that truth. I was happy and content to reside in a state of indecisiveness and continue to straddle the fence for as long as life would permit. However, that option was no longer available to me as she confronted me with the very question that I feared having to answer at the beginning of the journey. Sure, I could sustain not drinking alcohol, clubbing, listening to R&B and Hip-Hop and even not watching TV if I wanted. Those things were, for the most part, intimate to me unilaterally. In other words, my abstinence from them would not have any serious impact on anyone else's life. But, the no sex thing carried bilateral implications. By deciding to be celibate, I had effectively decided for Rian that she would adopt this lifestyle as well, whether she consented or not. The hard part for her, in my opinion, was not that she was opposed per se, but more related to the lack of voice she had in the decision. At any rate, I pondered over her question and I vacillated about going back into sexual sin for about a week or so, and then, I landed on a familiar side of the proverbial fence. Off went the clothing and I was back to my previous form.

At the time I found solace in that piece of conventional wisdom that said sex would be the "one" sin that God would have to deal with me on (as if I had no other sins that I consistently committed).

Did I feel bad about going back to a state of sexual

impurity? That is a tough question to answer. At the time I found solace in that piece of conventional wisdom that said sex would be the "one" sin that God would have to deal with me on (as if I had no other sins that I consistently committed). My convictions were still there, but I truly began to truly feel and believe that sex was an integral part of any vibrant and legitimate adult relationship. I also believed that as long as the two consenting adults were monogamous, there was no true harm being done to the world. After all, the thought of marriage had come across my mind a time or two with Rian, so I figured that this scenario was most representative of God's intent in the first place. As time progressed, I no longer struggled with my decision to have sex again. The questions surrounding it were far from my mind. In fact, habits in my life had returned to a place of comfort and familiarity. I was drinking alcohol, going to "lounges" (a nice compromise to the club right?), listening to R&B and Hip-Hop, watching TV and of course having sex. And church? Well, I still attended fairly regularly. In fact, Rian and I would go together from time to time. That said, while I may have physically been attending regularly, my mind would oftentimes be someplace else. I had fully regressed back to the person I was before the journey. What a waste of time?!

In the midst of all of this, Will and I began a real estate company, Theta Investments, LLC. The founding of this company was birthed from the multitude of frustrations we had experienced via corporate America. We often found ourselves unchallenged and under-utilized. As a result, we believed the solution to this problem was to start our own company. As roommates, we would often enjoy the nightlife in neighboring metropolitan hubs such as New York City, DC and the occasional trip back down to the Philadelphia area to link up with some of my old acquaintances. While we had a great social life, Theta Investments, LLC was our dream come true and a venture that we were very proud about. We purchased our first residential rehab project in the Germantown section of Philadelphia in the late summer of 2004. The house was a nice 2500 sq-ft property with 4 bedrooms and 1.5 bathrooms. Over the course of four months we worked tirelessly with various contractors and had the property completely rehabbed and ready to sell to a deserving homeowner. Though we experienced a few bumps and bruises throughout the process, we learned a great deal about life and real estate from the experience. Once the property rehab was completed, we worked with our realtor and put the property on the market for sale.

With my budding real estate business awaiting the sale of its first property, Rian and I thought it would be good to take a break and enjoy the holiday season. Since the conclusion of my 40-day journey and the decision to become sexually active again, Rian and I were enjoying one of the more pleasant stretches that our relationship had seen. Things were going really well. For Thanksgiving the previous year we had spent the day with my parents in my apartment in Lansdale. My mother cooked a big southern style turkey dinner for the four of us and we enjoyed the quiet ambiance that my suburban apartment provided. However, this year Rian suggested that we go to visit her family in Boston. I must admit, I was not particularly keen on the idea of going to Boston and missing my mom's Thanksgiving dinner, but I was willing to compromise. After all, Rian's family was cool, so I wasn't worried about feeling uncomfortable or out of place. With that in mind, we packed up and left New Jersey for the six hour ride to Boston.

The trip to Boston was a tumultuous one. The rain poured, fog thickened and thunder clapped for most of the journey. Thankfully, we arrived in one piece early in the morning around 4am. Due to fatigue and the hour of the night, we quietly eased our way into her aunt's house and went straight to our living quarters and immediately passed out. The next day, Rian and I went out to the mall and did some minor sightseeing around the Boston metro area. This was the first time I had visited a New England state and I was eager to get out and see what it had to offer. While in the mall, I picked up a book called, *The Seven Spiritual Laws of Success* by Deepak Chopra, which had been recommended to me by a mentor a few months before. When we returned to her aunt's house that afternoon, I began reading the book in search for the underlying character traits that were necessary to be successful with the motive of ensuring Theta Investments became a viable business entity. As I read the book, page by page, I was astounded at the bevy of knowledge contained therein. It was truly a page turner and by the time I had gotten to chapter 2, I knew that I would end up reading it straight through in one sitting. However, somewhere around the 4th chapter something odd happened that broke my concentration.

It was as if I heard the voice of God speak directly to me. At the time, I would not have considered myself overly spiritual, or, as some would call "a Jesus freak." Indeed, I loved the Lord, but I was still confused as to whether or not I was in love with Him. Nevertheless, He spoke to me that afternoon in Boston as I was reading. Here I was looking for the derivative of success and I was interrupted by God speaking about an entirely different aspect of life. "Be celibate for one year." That is what I heard. Now, one could argue that I did not hear that from the Lord and I would completely understand their cynicism. Truth be told, if you would have told me this part of the story 10 years ago, I would have been a bit cynical as well.

But yes, the Lord spoke to me. At the time, I did not clearly understand what this meant or even what the full purpose of the message was, but nonetheless I heard it. When I heard it, it was as if time stopped for a moment and all background noises were removed. I pinched myself to see if I was dreaming. No, I'm not. God had spoken to me.

In hearing what He said, I was at first a bit skeptical and honestly, stubborn to accept the reality of what I had been instructed to do. I was only a few months removed from the 40-day journey, which included celibacy, and I had no intention of becoming celibate for a one year period. Not only did I have no intention, but if I'm transparent, I had no interest in it either. And so, I sat on the couch with Chopra's book in hand and wrestled back and forth with what the Lord had said for a while – a long while. I tried my hardest to ignore what I heard, but it just would not go away. I tried to continue reading my book, but I was unable to focus. I even went into the room with Rian and the rest of her family, but I found myself aloof as the decision to obey or to disobey lay heavily on my heart. No matter how hard I tried, I was unable to block out or ignore God's instruction that evening.

After toiling over it for about two hours or so, I decided to call my fraternity brother Jason. Jason and I met in those first days at Howard. He and I had built a friendship based on similar principles and convictions. As a result, I knew I could count on Jason to understand the magnitude of what had occurred when God spoke to me celibacy. But, with this call I was not just looking for Jason's concurrence; I was also looking to engage Jason in the journey with me. So, I told Jason all about what had happened and this new conviction placed on me around being celibate for one year. While Jason was not as frivolous as I was when it came to sex, the call to be celibate for one year still presented a challenge for him. However, not to my surprise, he obliged and eagerly took on the challenge as he, too, had struggled internally for years with the conviction of sexual purity before God. Now would be his chance to once and for all renew his own commitment regarding that part of his life to God and obey His commands. I was elated because I knew that Jason would be able to stand strong and be the rock I needed in order to complete this new journey. I now had an accountability partner, but more importantly, another man of God who understood the purpose behind this new trek in life.

When I got off the phone with Jason, I called my friend, Nneka. Nneka had been a friend of mine since my intern days back in 2001. Our friendship, like mine with Jason, was built upon similar principles and belief in God's power. Back then, she was unknowingly responsible for keeping me connected with God as she took me and another intern back and forth to church on Sunday's when we had no car out there in the desolate town of Tarrytown, New York. When she answered the phone, I immediately in a school boys' zeal blurted out all that had happened and asked her if she would be willing to join me. At first she was a little resistant as she pondered over the unfortunate double standard of a celibate woman and its implications on relationships. Understanding the inherent challenges that she would face with the journey, I sought out to console and encourage her by passionately sharing again with her what God had laid on my heart. But this time I took aim at her spirit and heart as I knew both were full of God and that they would be more accepting of my request. With that appeal and God's nudging, it was not long before Nneka agreed and gladly accepted my invitation to take part in a one year journey of celibacy.

Though inconsistent with my faith, I indulged as often as possible as a sort of escape from my true self.

Ironically, when God first laid celibacy on my heart one of my biggest fears was the inherent loneliness of the journey. Being a member of a fraternity, graduate of an HBCU and man of middle-class stature, life had afforded me many sultry pleasantries. Though inconsistent with my faith, I indulged as often as possible as a sort of escape from my true self. In that indulgence, I met many friends and acquaintances, but never had in depth conversations with them to understand what lie beneath their social façade. As a result, I was not sure who would be around me when I took such a stand for an extended period of time based on what I believed was the right thing to do. It was in this very moment that I found myself very vulnerable. Looking back on it, I do not believe God would have had it any other way because my ego and pride had a historical trend of blocking out His will for my life. In my vulnerability, I was left to lean on Him and Him only. Thankfully, through my life He had introduced me to some pretty awesome people who loved Him just as much, if not more, than I did. True, all of us struggled with showing Him affection from time to time, but we had the fundamental components of love that would allow us to be led and used by Him. So, there we stood, Jason, Nneka and I, three peas in a pod, the three musketeers, three's a charm; ready to embark on a path to be close to the Lord, whose grace and mercy had protected us all throughout those wayward years.

Upon the initial conviction, just as I had rushed to tell Nneka and Jason, I also ran to inform Rian of this life-changing revelation. Surprisingly, she responded by telling me that she was not surprised. Really?! To her, she had seen this "next step" coming from a mile away. I was stunned. I thought to myself how I wished I could have seen it coming a mile away and if I had, how I might have behaved differently in the months preceding it. I would have at least sought out some exotic excursions to add more experiences to the sexual memory bank before my exile. But nonetheless, she saw it coming and astutely understood the implications on our relationship. Quietly, I was concerned about how our relationship would fare over the next few months because when I had previously abstained for 40 days, it appeared that we began to grow apart a little. How much more so would it be impacted after an entire year to boot? Did our relationship have the ingredients required to sustain itself in the absence of sex for such an extended period of time? Only time would tell and we both knew that it was going to be an interesting year because of it. In an attempt to hedge against future complications, we made a commitment to one another to proactively address issues whenever possible.

As stated, I was concerned about how Rian and I would fair this time around. We were just beginning to really hit a nice stride with our relationship and I was fearful that this new journey would abruptly disrupt our flow. Well, much to my chagrin, issues began before we even left Boston; the very weekend the journey began. The immediate issues escape my memory now, but I do remember that we commuted from Boston to New Jersey without speaking a single, solitary word. When we arrived in Jersey at my apartment to take a break, we began speaking and whatever chips that were on our shoulders seemed to have been removed. But, right as we were preparing to continue driving that day from New Jersey to DC, another argument ensued. A short, sharp dialogue erupted into a verbal tiff and lo and behold we were back to our voluntary solitary confinement.

We silently walked around the apartment, avoiding direct line of sight of one another, got our things together and headed out to DC to meet up with some friends for the remainder of the weekend. I was furious the whole ride down. I thought about how ridiculous it was for us to drive three hours, on top of the six from Boston, and not speak to each other. But in my own immaturity I was unwilling to break the ice. As I drove, I would occasionally glance to my right to observe Rian's cold stare into space as if I did not exist. It was really a sad day for our relationship. I had just recently, for the first time in my life, heard God speak directly to me. I was excited about what obedience to His call would bring about in my life. For once, I felt that I had a true sense of purpose in my life. Sure, maybe I had a sense of "meaning" before by the world's definition, but this was much different. I felt a new sense of accountability to the Lord and that accountability served as evidence of a relationship with Him. And through all of this, I was experiencing proverbial hell with my current relationship. Why?

When we arrived in DC, it still seemed as if the wounds

had not completely healed and so, I unsuccessfully tried to make light of the situation. Unfortunately, my humor only served to fuel the fire even more and eventually led to Rian putting me out of her apartment that night. See, I had already been banished from the bedroom because of the entire day's events. But, in the middle of the night, Rian walked out of the bedroom into the living room with tears streaming down her face and arms folded and told me that I needed to leave. This was a complete shock. She had never kicked me out. Not once. In fact, we had never slept anywhere but in the same bed (unless we were visiting with parents or vice-versa). Though I was very surprised by the magnitude to which the situation had escalated, there was a sense of peace that eventually covered me. I still to this day cannot explain why, but for some reason I did not even fight it. Maybe it was because the whole situation was a sign from above. Who knows? Whatever the reason, per her request, I packed up my bags and left her apartment having the sense that my exit symbolized more than just a physical egress.

As I drove over to a friend's house that night, I thought about what this incident would mean for the future of our relationship. I vividly remember calling Jason and Nneka the next day or so and explaining to them the events in real time in hopes of wisdom that would save my relationship. However, they both responded with the same response; a response that

I had begun to feel deep in my heart, but was not yet ready to accept as the true reality of my failed relationship. Rian and I had been together for almost two years at this point and a lot of time, energy and love had been invested. As a result, I was not willing to just throw in the towel without just cause. Nonetheless, Jason and Nneka both felt that the core issue with my relationship was the lack of equal yoking, meaning that Rian and I were spiritually on two different planes. Sigh... just cause.

I took some time over the next couple of days to reflect on what Jason and Nneka had said. Though they had never spoken to one another, I found it sheer irony that they both came to the same conclusion. Maybe it was divine intervention. Whatever it was, it sure wasn't coincidence. As I thought about what they said, I began to reminisce about my relationship with Rian. It appeared that from the moment I began reading *The Purpose Driven Life*, things began to change in our relationship. I became frustrated by the fact that there was no finger pointing in the world that could now help the situation. It wasn't her fault. It wasn't my fault. It wasn't anyone's fault. We were just on two different pages spiritually and as a result, there was no real opportunity for an amicable reconciliation. Ironically, it seemed as if things were just fine as sex abode unquestioned in our relationship in the absence of any sort of spiritual conviction. We got along well and had tons of fun together. But, as soon as sex found itself on the altar as part of my journey, our relationship began to change. Consequently, it appeared that the sexual impurity in our relationship had served as a relational veneer that occluded us from more fully seeing and learning who we were individually. The truth is that as my journey unfolded, I began to change and before long, the person that Rian came to know by the end of 2004 was not the same person that she entered into a relationship with in 2003. These things being considered, I decided, in the best interest of both Rian and I, to end things before someone got hurt even further. In essence, I too had come to the conclusion that we truly weren't equally yoked.

Ironically, it seemed as if things were just fine as sex abode unquestioned in our relationship in the absence of any sort of spiritual conviction.

The break-up with Rian left me with mixed emotions. On the one hand, I was relieved that it was finally over and that I would no longer have to fight with her (we had gotten pretty snarky with one another at the tail end of the relationship). But, on the other hand, I was sad because I really cared for her. And though I concluded that in the end we weren't equally yoked, a part of me believed that with time, Rian would have "gotten there" and joined me on the same page in my spiritual walk. However, I also knew that if this were going to happen, it would not be because of something I did. It would be the Lord's work. I never doubted that she didn't care for me, but no matter how much she cared, she couldn't become a "new" person to meet the needs that I now had. In fact, even if she would have, I'm confident that we would have still arrived at the same place because she wouldn't have been true to herself. At the end of the day, both of us had to come to grips with who we were, though that person might have evolved over time, and decide whether or not our relationship "fit" anymore.

For me, the decision was no. I don't know if she concluded the same thing at the time, but I do know that she was unwilling to "fake it" and thus, there was not any feasible way we could have continued moving forward. Ironically, as time passed, I found myself missing her and questioning my decision. In fact, there were a few occasions over the next year or so where I tried to stir things back up to see if "it" was still there. Maybe part of it was because I did not have anyone else and I was fearful of being lonely. Maybe, just maybe, it was because I was selfish and couldn't accept a reality where someone else would "have" her as their own. While I'm not entirely clear on what drove this remorseful behavior, it did not matter because my attempts were unsuccessful. Whether she was preoccupied with someone else or if after talking a few times we realized the "magic" that once took up residence was no longer there, we both eventually came to the sobering reality that our story had finally come to a close.

One cold, windy afternoon in early 2005, shortly after the new year had begun, I received a call from Jason. At this point, we had been on our celibacy journey for a little over a month and a half. We did our normal salutations, but I could tell that something was on his mind. When I inquired further, he began to tell me a story of how he had fallen off the wagon. He said that he tried to resist, but it was just too difficult and he succumbed to the desires of his flesh not even two months into our journey. I was devastated! Jason was my spiritual rock. I looked to him in times when I was weak and from my viewpoint, I perceived him to be much further along in his journey with Christ than I was. He was supposed to be there for me when I came to him with news that I had fallen. *Come on!* This news of him having sex couldn't have been more startling, but yet revealing of the true power that sin can have over one's life. While I wanted to be mad at him, I could not fault or blame Jason for I didn't know how much longer I myself would last. In fact, there really was not much at all that I could say. Scolding would have done no good, because Jason was clear on the purpose of the commitment. He knew that he did not have to answer to me; he had to answer to God. So, we just sat there on the phone silent. The silence caused anxiety and both of us wanted to say something but were at a loss for words. Then it dawned on me; the conviction around sexual sin was placed on me. And as much as I wanted to push it off onto others, I would ultimately be held responsible for seeing it through. Not Jason. Not Nneka. Though I had two friends who committed to take part in the journey with me, I could not allow myself to become side tracked by their "performance" or "non-performance" along the way. Jason broke the silence with a charge to me to continue the journey strong and he let me know that he would continue to be by my side every step of the way.

After Jason's news, I have to admit that I was a bit discouraged. I began to second guess if I had really heard God speak to me that November in Boston. Many of my friends who I had told about my decision were supportive, but jokingly expressed their unwillingness to fight this fight. Interestingly enough, I couldn't blame them for that stance as the thought of continuing another ten months seemed an impossible and daunting task. Before long, I started to feel alone and isolated because I had no other male who could empathize with the emotional turmoil associated with the journey. Yes, Jason was still on board, however, with his step backwards I felt that he could no longer relate to what I was going through. And Nneka was there two, but she was a female and her experiences and context were different than mine. In this weakened state, with no one to turn to, the only thing that I could do was pray. And pray I did.

For the next month or so, Jason and I would share stories of our journey with one another. Although Jason had fallen early in the journey, his daily struggles and frustrations were not too different from mine. We would talk about the women that we were dating. We would discuss the challenges resulting from our declaration of celibacy and more specifically, those moments when we wanted to throw in the towel. We encouraged one another to stay strong and keep up the good fight. Originally, I believed that because of his sampling of the forbidden fruit more recently than I had, he would not truly be able to relate. But as time progressed, I stood corrected as I witnessed his struggles entangled with his sincere desire to please God. Nneka, on the other hand, appeared to be cruising. I guess the initial months were not that difficult for her, as women historically tend to wait a bit longer before they allow sex to enter a relationship in the first place. Additionally, most women view sex as a sacred activity, and as such, revere it much higher than their male counterparts. In discussions with her, these two rationales were validated as she expressed her concern for the latter months in the journey and the potential impacts of a tenured boyfriend. But, nonetheless, she was standing strong as well. And so, we pressed on, towards our goal.

By the late spring of 2005, Theta Investments was up

and running full steam ahead. Will and I had successfully flipped our first property in the late winter and we had developed a strategy to reinvest the profits back into the business. As such, we sought out additional residential real estate to acquire. Because we were so intent on real estate being our way out of corporate America, we decided that an investment mix of rental properties and rehab projects would best accelerate our exit timeline due to the opportunity for both profitability and sustainability. The challenge, however, in achieving this goal was that we did not have the funds to pursue it in its entirety. The profits from our first project would have lent themselves well toward a rental property or rehab project, but not both. Due to the absence of funds needed to successfully implement our planned strategy, we developed a private investor program and sought out investors who would be willing to infuse capital into our dream and assist in our financial objectives.

Now, I was no finance guru and neither was Will, but we had groomed ourselves well through associations with real estate tycoons, bankers, realtors and the likes, all in hopes of plugging the gaps of our financial deficiency. Not long after that, we began seeking seed money from friends and family to build the capital necessary to continue the pursuit of our dream. All in all, over the course of about three or so months we raised a significant amount of working capital, far exceeding the amount we needed to move the business forward. Honestly, while our private investor program contained the appropriate incentives to entice investment, no one invested in Theta Investments because of our financial prowess or the robust business model we presented them with; they invested because they believed in us. Again, these were friends and family, and many of them had the opportunity to witness us grow and develop over the years into respectable young men who had stayed out of trouble. It was that familiarity that allowed them to feel comfortable supporting us, though the dream was aggressive, in our endeavors.

With the capital acquired from our seed rounds and profits from the first project we flipped, we were ready to move forward. We were feeling pretty good about ourselves at the time, blessed even. And as the hubris began to settle in, our eyes became bigger than our intellect and discernment. Ego-based decision-making began to replace prudent, "measure twice, cut once" decision-making. As a result, over the course of the next three months we purchased four properties. Two of the properties were rentals and the remaining two were residential rehabs. It seemed as if our strategy was in full effect and we were well on our way to profitability and sustainability, ultimately with an end goal of being able to leave the mundane tasks of the corporate environment. While the strategy was now operational, there was a looming question that persisted. Had we done too much too quick? We had only completed one residential rehab prior to that time. An argument can be made that real estate was hot at the time and there really weren't any "bad" buys around. In fact, within a month of closing on a property, it was highly likely that you would have achieved some amount of equity because of the bullish market conditions. Though those arguments would be sound, it is my belief that our purchases were draped in our own egos and we sought success and status more than achievement. We wanted to get rich quick. Unfortunately for us, our pursuit of riches and status ended up crippling the business before it even got a firm footing established.

By the fall of 2005, we were juggling multiple responsibilities across all four properties. All of them needed some degree of work and as such, we had to develop a contractor team. I am reluctant to say that the process of finding good work was easy by the least bit. After being burned, both financially and from a schedule/timing perspective, we finally found a guy that we could trust. And trust we did, as we relied heavily on him to not only complete the tasks he had been assigned, but also to clean up the mess that the other contractors left behind. By the time November had arrived, we were ready to rent out one of the two rentals (Kolhan Road - the other rental was a Section 8 in which we inherited tenants upon settlement) and put one of the two residential rehabs, Thompson Street, on the market for sale. The other rehab project, Milken Street, was not ready for sale yet due to some scheduling delays and the size of the renovation. But, we were accepting of that reality because it was going to be our ticket out; our silver bullet. Milken Street had the highest upside and would allow us to not only pay all private investors back, but it was expected to provide us with a nice profit margin in order to continue and grow operations. With its rehab still underway, we began aggressively working with our realtor to get Thompson Street sold and Kolhan Road rented.

Anyone could tell you that one of the worst times to have a property on the market for rent and sale is during the holidays. Most people looking to buy/rent do not want to break up their child's school year in the middle and typically people do not like to move in the winter months. Sure, this was conventional wisdom, but what could we do about the cards we had been dealt? Our desire was to have the properties on the market earlier, but illegitimate contractors and some bad management on our part had pushed our timelines back. Regardless, we were fairly confident that we would be able to sell Thompson Street and get tenants into the 3-story duplex at Kolhan Road. By late November, we had found tenants for the bottom unit of Kolhan road, but still struggled to find someone for the top unit. As we continued to seek out tenants for that vacant unit, Thompson St. sat idle with very few showings at all.

Right after the first of the year I received a call from my realtor saying that someone had broken into Thompson Street. I was in shock. I quickly drove over to see the damage to find that the back door frame had been broken, two windows were broken, the vanity in the bathroom was gone and all of the copper piping throughout the house had been stolen. The theft had pretty much reversed the very work that we had completed to get the property into shape to sell. I dialed Will's number on my cell phone as I stood in the center of the living room in disbelief and gave him the news. After we spoke, I called our insurance agent to let him know, only to find out that we did not have theft or vandalism insurance. Wow. As I had my contractor secure the broken door with nails and board the windows up, I thought to myself, "This can't be happening to me." As a result of the break-in, we had to re-rehab the property, which would further delay our timeline for selling.

With news of Thompson Street being broken into still fresh on our minds, Will and I began to have doubts about our endeavors. It was very challenging to manage the properties while still carrying full-time jobs and the demands seemed to be growing by the day. As we began to figure out how we would finance the repairs for Thompson Street, we were also faced with the quagmire of carrying two-thirds of the mortgage for Kolhan Road due to its continued vacancy in the top 3 bedroom unit. Before long, we were carrying two full mortgages, Thompson St. and Milken St., and two-thirds of another in that of Kolhan Rd. To say that these properties were becoming a serious financial burden is an understatement. Sure, we had good paying jobs, but they really only supported our own mortgages and subsequent lifestyles. And although we were very conservative in our own spending/budgeting habits, the cost of living in the Philadelphia, PA and Somerset, NJ areas was quite expensive for recent college graduates. Through credit cards and personal/business loans, we were able to find a way to stay afloat. No sooner than when we had managed to refrain from sinking into the financial abyss did news of a real estate bubble and its projected burst begin to headline all media circuits.

By the time the spring arrived, it was obvious that a vacation was needed. The stress and burden of Theta Investment's woes had begun weighing heavily on me. In fact, the amount of fires that we had to put out from late 2005 to this point in 2006 had consumed me so, that I had hardly realized that my one year goal of celibacy had been achieved. I could not believe that it had been about 15 months or so and I was not dying to jump back into the throes of sexual immorality. Honestly, the thought to or not to have sex had not really crossed my mind much at all. I was too distracted with trying to keep Theta Investments afloat. And unfortunately, I had no clear future direction with which to focus my journey of celibacy on going forward. My commitment to God was for one year per His request and since the year had long passed, I did not know what to do next.

As I reflected on the last 15 months of celibacy I began to draw a startling correlation. It seemed odd to me that before I started the journey, Theta Investments was well on its way, but almost identically coinciding with the end of year one, things began rapidly spiraling down. This was startling because I was under the impression that if I stopped having sex that God would instantly bless me. After all, when I was having sex

> *This was startling because I was under the impression that if I stopped having sex that God would instantly bless me.*

I was blessed; so I was sure that the blessings would now far exceed what I could imagine. But, that is not what happened at all. In actuality, the exact opposite had occurred. And as a result, to be completely honest, I felt that God had betrayed me. I was familiar with the Bible's saying that "He will never forsake or leave you," but that was no consolation for the emotions and experience I was having at the time. Fortunately for me, I would be able to put all of this behind me as I geared up for my vacation with my boys from college to Rio de Janeiro,

Brazil.

I was very excited as this would be my first trip out of the country necessary of a passport. That evening as I packed my bags, many thoughts began racing through my head. I wondered what Rio would be like and if it was as bad as everyone said it was. See, of all the people I had known who had been to Rio, the one thing they talked about when they got back was the women. Not the sights, the culture or the food, but the women and the abundance and availability thereof. And even though I was still running on fumes with my celibacy walk, I had somehow convinced myself that a trip to Rio did not necessarily have to coincide with sexual conquests with women.

I also thought to myself about Theta Investments and how I would need to get on the grind when I got back into the country. By this time, Milken St. was on the market, but had not yet sold. On the other hand, Thompson St. had not been repaired yet from the previous break-in due to lack of financing. One glimmer of hope was that Kolhan Rd. was finally fully rented out and the second rental property still remained without issue. Unfortunately, the speculated real estate bubble had indeed burst and we were faced with the quagmire of what to do with our two properties, Thompson and Milken. Should we rent them out? Should we sell under value and take a loss? All of these were thoughts regarding

Theta Investments that consumed my mind as I tried to clear my head in preparation for my vacation.

And lastly, the woman I was dating at the time crossed my mind. In fact, as I packed, I was waiting for her to come by to help later that evening. I wondered if we would become an item at some point in the future. I had not seriously dated anyone since Rian. As such, most of my celibate dating life was filled with various women from different places. I must admit, initially, I found the dating scene very challenging as a celibate male. As I met different women, I would usually be intentionally ambiguous whenever the topic of dating, ex's and sex would come up. I wasn't ashamed per se, but I was afraid that too much "God" talk (celibacy rings of "holier than thou") early on would ruin any chance I had at getting past a first date. Interestingly enough, whenever I successfully got past that first date and would engage in conversations that called for a bit more substance, there were a few women that found it hard to accept the fact that I was not having sex. Some of them took it personal as if I was on some type of male empowerment (or female disempowerment) trip. Others, I suppose, found it unattractive and slowly, but surely, exited stage left. To the contrary, there were others who were thrilled and thought of me as a godsend. I thrived off this cohort and in some twisted way, found a way to turn the attention that my celibate walk received away from God and onto myself. Unfortunately, that same ego that had grown in my collegiate days was awoken by the praise received and would soon enough rear its ugly head. And then there were those who were cynical about the whole thing and tested and tried me to see if I would fall. I found humor in their attempts, but in similar fashion, they too fed my ego in their aggressive pursuit of trying to get me to fall. Nevertheless, after dating a few women here and there, I ended up meeting Chelsea and she was a pretty cool girl. We connected on a couple of levels, but the one in which I found mildly refreshing was spiritually. Chelsea and I had met sometime in March, but we began dating in April and here we were in June as a pretty consistent couple with no strings attached.

As you can see, there were a multitude of issues, concerns, fears, inquiries and ideas that were going through my head at the time; all of them to be confronted when I touched down back in the US at the conclusion of my trip. And though Rio had been dubbed as the ultimate "mancation" for debauchery of all sorts, I was just seeking some rest and relaxation. I was truly looking forward to the opportunity to disconnect from the world for a seven day stretch. Surprisingly, by the time we boarded the plane in Philadelphia, headed for Miami for our connecting flight, many of my worries had begun to subside. I walked down the center aisle and found my row and slid into my window seat. Within a few minutes all passengers were aboard and the safety presentation was complete. As the airplane began taxing down the runway, I found myself falling asleep as I leaned against the window sill. Before I fully lost consciousness, I remember reflecting on the past 18 month celibate journey. In similar fashion to that of the first 40-day journey, I wondered if anything had been achieved. I also thought about the plethora of opportunities that would exist in Rio and whether or not I would partake. After all, I had made it for the full year. What was I still holding out for? Before I had the chance to fully vet these thoughts, I was asleep...

4

ROAD TO SUBMISSION

Romans 6:19 – "I put this in human terms because you are weak in your natural selves. Just as you used to offer the parts of your body in slavery to impurity and to ever-increasing wickedness, so now offer them in slavery to righteousness leading to holiness."

Early that morning, as we rode in the taxi back to the airport in Rio de Janeiro, Brazil, I was filled with intense guilt and remorse. My plan to enjoy the vacation without distraction had pretty much failed as soon as I landed. I would like to blame it on peer pressure, but unfortunately, that was not the case. Thinking back, there was a sense of rebelliousness that fueled my behavior over the course of that week; an oddly placed sense of retribution for the "wrong" that God had bestowed upon me. But, I was no more whole on the ride back to the airport than I was when I left the states. I believe, subconsciously, I thought that by acting in direct opposition to God's will I would have freed myself from the frustration and stress that had compounded over the 18 months leading up to the trip. Though a myriad of thoughts

...there was a sense of rebelliousness that fueled my behavior over the course of that week; an oddly placed sense of retribution for the "wrong" that God had bestowed upon me.

and ideologies drove me to a shameful state of behavior while in Brazil, I now had to live with it as a reality because the fantasy was over.

To think, I had gone 18 long months without having sex. What an accomplishment? I did not feel that way. Many of the friends around me heralded my achievement as if I had done some noble thing. So much so, there was a point where I began to indulge in their praise and think more of myself than I should have. But, I did not feel like a champion when I landed in the Philadelphia airport after the trip. In fact, I felt a deep sense of isolation come upon me. I did not really want to talk much about the trip and did not want to do much of anything. I had mixed emotions about what I had done. A part of me felt as if I had blown it. God had called me to a higher standard of living and at the first sight of trials, I ran in the opposite direction. But another, more arrogant, part of me found relief in the thought that I had gone longer than most without sex. It was an unrealistic and dated expectation anyway, right? For the sake of getting back on my feet quickly and removing the tail from between my legs, I chose to side with the arrogant side of me and discounted the sins of the trip as trivial as a little white lie.

God had called me to a higher standard of living and at the first sight of trials, I ran in the opposite direction.

When I finally arrived home, I checked my mail and had received something from Wachovia, which was the bank that held the Theta Investments business account. I was a bit concerned as I had already received the account statement before the trip. So, I had no idea what the envelope could have contained. Once I opened it I realized that it was a returned rent check for the top floor of Kolhan Road. I immediately called the tenant and informed her of the situation. She went back and forth about how she was having a hard time and that she would not be able to pay it all, but would be willing to pay half now and then the other half in two weeks. Some would call my response to her situation naïve, but I have always been empathetic with people and I typically give everyone the benefit of the doubt; the first time around. So, after hearing her story I agreed to allow her to split the payments up and we met to exchange the first installment shortly thereafter. When the time had come for the 2nd installment, I did not hear from her. I called and left numerous messages and still no response. Finally, I went by and inquired about the rent and she became very defensive and said that it was on the way. Again, I waited and to no avail, the rent check never came. After Will and I discussed the matter, we decided it was time to evict her. Once we completed filling out the initial paperwork we found out that the eviction would take about three to four months. Unfortunately, with the burdens resulting from the other properties that were sitting idle on the market, we did not have the ability to carry that portion of the mortgage for longer than two months. We had no idea of what to do.

At the same time, Thompson St was still in need of repair. As we began to have contractors visit to inspect the damage, we found out that even more work was needed than we originally thought. A new heating unit and roof would be needed if we were going to be able to rent it out and cover the mortgage. While the costs of that option were high, the market for a house with a bum heater was even lower which would have ultimately caused the house to continue to sit on the market. As a result, we decided that we had no other option than to repair it once again with all the trimmings so that we would be in the position to either sell or rent, whichever came first. This renovation put us even further into an already red hole and completely stretched us to our financial limits. In the end, every line of credit, credit card and business loan we had was completely out. We had almost quadruple the amount of money going out each month as we did coming in. We were quickly approaching bankruptcy as an option both as a company and personally.

Will and I were furious. At who? I'm not sure. While in my own fury, I began to wonder if somehow my actions in Brazil had anything to do with our current distress. Sure there were challenges before I left, but upon arrival back in the states things had gone completely haywire. The more I thought about that being a possibility, the angrier I became about the situation and God. I felt it if this were the case, it was unjust judgment on me. Surely my 18 months of sacrifice were worthy of protection from such distress. And what about Will? Was he reaping from what I sowed? That didn't seem equitable. I was truly speechless. How did everything get so bad so quick? What did I do to deserve this? My dreams were truly shattering before my eyes and my confidence in my own abilities right along with them.

By the time October of 2006 had arrived, we had finished the eviction process at Kolhan. The noise around Theta Investments had quieted down a bit, but still no financial relief. With no apparent out, I did what most "good" Christians do; I decided on one Sunday to go to church. I had gone to this particular church a few times before in the past, but had never joined. At this point in my life I had a somewhat jaded view of religion and was not sure where I stood or whether or not church in the religious sense was necessary for a relationship with Christ. But, in this time of deep despair, and with no answers to resolve the situation, I knew nowhere else to turn but to God and the church. Now, I was still upset with Him, but I knew deep down inside that it would only be by His grace that I would get out of this situation. As I sat there that Sunday in the back of the church, the Word moved with mighty power. Service was fantastic and I found it hard to stay in my seat when the doors of the church were opened for new members, but I was not ready to commit to church or God again yet. It had been almost two years since I had really been active with church and as a result, I was in no hurry to jump back in. As far as God, I had seen where submitting to Him had gotten me via the situation at the time, so I was not too trusting of conceding to Him either. Additionally, there was still a part of me that desired to leave the door open for sex. Not that I necessarily wanted to have sex with anyone in particular, but my flesh relished in the availability of that as an option. And I knew, if I got back involved with church, it would become difficult for me to revel in that specific sin ever again.

And I knew, if I got back involved with church, it would become difficult for me to revel in that specific sin ever again.

A week had passed since I had gone to church, and it was time to decide if I would go again. Not much had changed over the course of the week, but something inside urged me to go. With no distractions in my life at the time, I decided to yield to this urging and go. Once more, the word was powerful and moving and I felt convicted to join, but I fought hard during the invitation to discipleship to remain in my seat. As the pastor stated that familiar inquisition about the possibility that there is still one who has not come down yet, I sat still almost frozen completely. Although I did not budge during service, as soon as church was over, I went to the back with the deacons and joined the church that day in October 2006. Little did I know that God's hand had been at work in my life the entire time, even through the tribulations, and that He would begin to reveal His purpose for it all very soon.Interestingly enough, after joining church that day, I felt that my days of sexual immorality were numbered and that it would soon no longer be "acceptable" sin for me. And sure enough, not long after I joined did the original call of celibacy return, but this time there was no timeline attached. God was again looking for me to live a life of celibacy until marriage. And now that he had my undivided attention through the trials and tribulations of Theta Investments, He sought to teach and show me things that would become instrumental in re-establishing my body as a temple of His and ultimately living a life consistent with His will.

5

RENEWAL

Romans 12:2 – "Do not conform any longer to the pattern of this world, but be transformed by the renewing of your mind. Then you will be able to test and approve what God's will is – his good, pleasing and perfect will."

I suppose the first time I encountered celibacy as part of my quest to find my purpose and fulfill a void within via the *Purpose Driven Life*, I was somewhat naïve and uninformed. So much so, that it wasn't until about 5 or 6 months after my awakening that day (when I joined my new church home) that this awareness became embarrassingly evident. Within a matter of minutes, all of the effort that I had prided myself on during the celibate journey had been distilled down to nothing more than an act of personal discipline and elective choice rather than spiritual obedience. My reality was shattered and I thought that I would never be able to show my face in public again. See, I had become somewhat of a "model" for celibacy within my circle of friends and as a result, many people viewed the celibate lifestyle as synonymous with my daily living. It is true that I found joy in this reality. In part because I believed that in my celibate walk people were given a glimpse of what God was about, but also because it made me somewhat of an enigma. But on this day, all of that would be shattered and I would be left to pick up the pieces and search for a new way forward.

I was dating a woman by the name of Tasha at the time when this truth came to light. She was the first woman that I had seriously dealt with since my renewed commitment to celibacy. Interestingly enough, Tasha was not a Christian. Sure, she went to church from time to time and spoke passionately about who God was in relation to her own life, but she had not declared Jesus Christ as her personal Lord and Savior. As I look back on it, I'm not sure why this was the case and I found it surprising. Tasha was older than me, about 8 years my senior. And though there was a significant age gap, we clicked very well. I'd always been told that I was an "old soul" and maybe that was the reason. But, whatever the case, I was just excited to have finally have met a woman who accepted not only who I was, but also the journey that I was on.

When we first met, I have to admit, I tried to run game on Tasha. We were at a social event and I made a pass at getting her number. Not surprisingly, she eluded my advance and made mention of the fact that maybe we'd meet again if it were "meant to be." And so, I went on about my business and within a matter of a few weeks, we ran into each other again at a Christmas event. Now, I've never subscribed to lightning striking twice, but in this instance I reveled at its possibility. When our eyes met, there was a cynical look on her face and I was intrigued to go and investigate. We chatted for a few moments and I persisted with where I left off during our last encounter. This time she obliged, however, providing me with her business card without the luxury of any personal information. I took this as a challenge and before long we were emailing back and forth daily. Shortly after that, we were going on the occasional date and before long we were somewhat of an item – courting some would say.

On this particular evening, Tasha and I were sitting in my living room discussing faith and in particular celibacy. She was intrigued by my transparency and also my commitment and as someone who hadn't quite figured the whole "God" thing out (not that I had either), she looked to me as a source of information and clarity. As such, on this evening while we were discussing celibacy she thought it wise to understand more about what the word meant and what the journey entailed. In response to her inquisition, I provided her with about as much depth as one can gain from Merriam-Webster and as a result, she probed further. Specifically, she was looking to understand how celibacy played itself out in my life, with particular focus on dating. To take it one step further, she wanted to know what lines of intimacy, if any, did I cross? I found her inquisitiveness cute and eagerly responded to each full of confidence. As it related to intimacy, I told her that to be celibate meant that one did not have sex. In response, she inquired about where foreplay came into the picture. Was it or was it not fair game? Irrationally exuberant, I replied that it was in fact fair game and that as long as you didn't have sex you were good to go. No sooner did the words leave my mouth did her countenance drop in bewilderment. Confused as to the origin of this change in disposition, I asked her what was wrong. With that, she burst out laughing. I couldn't figure out what was going on, so I joined in. After a moment or so, she gathered herself together and declared that what I had described couldn't possibly be celibacy. How could foreplay be fair game and qualify one as righteous when many of its activities were just as lascivious? She informed me that she thought the whole point of celibacy was to grow closer to God through restraint of sexual perversion and yet, my activities embraced all of them except one – sex. I was in complete shock and embarrassment. I had no response.

> *How could foreplay be fair game and qualify one as righteous when many of its activities were just as lascivious?*

Truthfully, it was as if she had put a mirror up to my face and shown me truth versus reality and the reflection was not pretty. What had I been thinking?! All this time, during the 40-day journey, during the 1-year period? I had boldly proclaimed celibacy to anyone that would listen and yet my very actions contradicted that which I proclaimed. I had never been so embarrassed in my life. I thought about how misplaced my anger had been in those times where I believed that God had unjustly rained misfortune on me, especially during the Theta Investment days. I thought about how cocky I had gotten in my own walk; so much so that I was celibate more so for personal challenge than in response to God's command. While embarrassment was the emotion I most felt at the time, the reality of the situation is that I had been humbled. Here I sat in conversation with someone who was not even a Christian and yet, they had the divine wisdom to see that my walk was nothing but a façade. I never thought that a non-Christian could put me in my place, but Tasha did. In fact, she unknowingly taught me the lesson that God can (and will) use anyone to speak to His children. And in this instance, He spoke loudly and forcefully.

> *I thought about how cocky I had gotten in my own walk; so much so that I was celibate more so for personal challenge than in response to God's command.*

As much as I wanted to tuck my tail and run, I had to face this situation head on because within a month of the conversation that Tasha and I had, I would be presenting a workshop on celibacy to a group of young men as part of a community outreach program. As a result, there would be no time for bitterness or indecisiveness. For it was clear now what my journey was to entail. No more fondling, no more tongue-kissing, no more sleeping in the same bed; basically, no more sexual contact period. It was that simple. It was never more complicated, but I suppose my own limited knowledge allowed me to find rectitude in a false and incomplete understanding of God's Word. In order to move forward, I would have to treat each woman as though she were the sister in Christ that God had intended her to be. This would indeed be a paradigm shift for me, but I had no choice. I knew that I loved God and upon learning that my actions beforehand were inconsistent with His will, I had to respond in obedience. Through this experience, my mind had truly been renewed.

> *No more fondling, no more tongue-kissing, no more sleeping in the same bed; basically, no more sexual contact period. It was that simple.*

The celibacy workshop went better than I expected and I suppose that my transparency and newly found humility is what led to the great flow of information that occurred between me and the participants. It was one of the most fulfilling things that I had ever done in my life. The peace and joy that surrounded the workshop was unlike any that I had ever experienced. And for that moment in time, I was genuinely happy. No gaping hole within to fill. No yearning for something more. I felt that I had finally identified what my purpose was and I was overjoyed with emotion. I was walking in the will of God.

To celebrate the success of the workshop, Tasha and I went out to one of our favorite spots. At this point, she and I had been dating consistently for about 5 months. While she was responsible for my awakening of sorts as it related to celibacy, she never held that experience against me. More importantly, Tasha had recently accepted Christ and was slated to be baptized later that May. So, things were going really well between us. As far as the "true" celibacy journey, things were going well with that as well. For Tasha, it was a bit of a challenge, because she had never thought of herself as someone that would be celibate. Sure, she had accepted that there would be dry spells in her adult life where she would not be sexually active for an extended period of time, but the choice of celibacy, before me, had never crossed her mind. Even still, she was strong and fully on board with me in the journey and as a result, our relationship grew stronger over the months.

Around the sixth month of our relationship, something began to weigh heavily on my spirit. Again, Tasha and I were doing very well with the celibate journey and as a result, this was my first relationship without sex ever being an object of focus at some point. Even though we began dating while I was still confused as to what celibacy was, I had never crossed the fence and thus, at this point we were engaged in a "pure" relationship. However perfect things seemed to be, there was still something burdening me heavily. I tried to ignore it, but it became heavier and heavier each and every passing day. At first I wasn't sure what it was, but over time it became clear. I was struggling to accept Tasha's age. While an 8 year age difference wouldn't be considered that large by most, for me, I became concerned about what our future would look like as a result. For example, I wanted to have kids; at least three or four. Seeing that Tasha was 34 at the time, this goal would become extremely challenging for us unless we were to begin right away. And right away was something that I was unable to commit to at the time. I liked Tasha a lot and felt that we had a good thing going, but because of her age and possibly my immaturity, I was unable to embrace a true future with her. I could not get over this hump and as a result, I was forced to do something that I had never done before.

Usually when I broke up with someone it was because of a legitimate (at least in my eyes) reason. This reason was oftentimes found layered in the frustration of the "moment" and thus, my decision would be extremely easy. However, with Tasha it was different. I had no frustrations or specific annoyances with her in the moment at hand. In fact, at the time, things could not have been better. But, the reality was that in my heart of hearts, I knew that I would never be able to accept her age; the very thing that she could not change.

It wasn't as if she had aged 8 years from when we began dating till now, so why now had it become a problem? I struggled with an answer to this question for awhile before one came to me. In my past relationships, they were so mired in sexual perversion that many of the substantive things would often go unaddressed. However, in my situation with Tasha, because we were actively practicing celibacy, the time spent together translated into much more value. And as I came to understand this, I recognized that the cruelest act that I could commit towards her would be to waste her time. As a result, I expelled a lot of energy truly assessing whether or not there could be a "we" in the future. Every time I would think on the matter, things would sway in favor of yay until I would reach her age as I scrolled through the list of attributes. Is it possible that with time I could have gotten over it? Sure. But, because I was undecided, I owed it to her to not take up any more of her precious invaluable time with my indecisiveness.

Consequently, I eventually went to Tasha to explain all of this to her. I have to admit, it was a very tough conversation to have, but one that had to occur. While she did not take it particularly well, she did acknowledge her appreciation for my honesty. Frankly, that was all I could hope for and it provided me some solace. When she exited the car after our discussion concluded, I sat in her driveway overwhelmed by emotion. What had I done? Was she the "one" for me? Was she placed in my life to be my "Proverbs 31" woman (you know... the "virtuous woman")? Had I just let her go over something trivial? As these questions raced through my mind, my eyes began to water and eventually I felt the warm, slow trickle of a tear escape from my eye and eventually land on my shirt. Without Tasha, I was now single again and as a result, would be forced to enter the dating world as a celibate, fully celibate, young man. To say the least, I knew the future would be both challenging and interesting.

In the first few months after Tasha and I ended our relationship, I found myself getting much more active at my church. My involvement had begun to pick up a bit earlier in the year, but without a "relationship" to focus on, I found myself being more intentional about occupying my time and mind with the things of God. Somewhat to my surprise, I found participation in the various ministries at my church very fulfilling. While some served me directly in strengthening my spiritual health by engaging the Bible in ways that my own independent study did not offer, others did so indirectly by providing me the opportunity to practice selflessness and be of service to others. I had found myself a nice little groove and it felt good. I was meeting new people through my participation and even getting opportunities to lead in some instances. I felt that God was really using me and it was an exciting period of time for me. As I had heard it mentioned many times before, singleness is a gift and so, I tried hard to make sure that I accepted this season of my life as such and allow God to do what He chose with me.

Though ministry brought me great fulfillment and occupied much of my time in those days, I still came home each evening to the more sobering side of singleness. You know the reality right? The one in which you enter a quiet house at night with no one waiting with open arms to greet you. And, the one that has you eating dinner (for me, this would oftentimes be a Stouffers, Swanson or Hungryman special) by yourself. Or, the one that has you watching your favorite television show with a bag of popcorn in the company of me, myself and I. At times, I enjoyed these realities. I found them freeing and enjoyed the opportunity to reflect and engage in introspection without distraction. In fact, I'm thankful because this solitude provided me the environment that allowed me to reconcile many of the issues of the day. However, if I'm honest, there were times where these same realities frustrated me; even more so in the context of my desire to live a celibate lifestyle.

It was one thing to strive towards celibacy in a relationship, especially one that involves two parties completely sold out for Christ and the cause. My relationship with Tasha had shown me that. However, it was completely another thing to do so and be single in the over-sexualized society of today. As a result, in those same months where I found participation in ministry fulfilling, I silently wrestled with this more cruel side of my singleness and was having a rough time. Though some of the difficulties were similar to that which I had experienced in the past, the fact that I now had a full understanding of what celibacy meant brought new complexities to this reality. With the passing of each month, I found myself growing more and more lonely. In an attempt to take control of the situation since God was taking too long, I tried a hand at getting back with Leann. Yes, Leann! But, as you might expect, it didn't work and so, I ended up right back where I was – lonely. In this state of solitude I found myself once again struggling with sexual sin, but this time it was sin against self in that of masturbation. Yes, it too was wrong and not acceptable in God's eyes. And though I knew this and had taught it in workshops, I still had to fight to resist the urge to please myself in the absence of the options I had in the past. To try to reduce these feelings of loneliness, I'd hit up my boys from time to time in search of male camaraderie as an outlet. We would kick it and have a good time and it would satiate me for a time. But unfortunately, those good times still didn't replace the company of a woman. As a result, I realized that I would at some point have to begin dating again. And since the retry with Leann had already been unsuccessful, I would have to step outside of my comfort zone and meet women who I did not know.

Ironically, I ran into some resistance when it came to the dating scene as a result of being a celibate male. See, within the traditional Christian paradox, most people have easily come to accept celibate females as a result of their understanding of "preservation-ism" in light of chastity. Therefore, celibacy amongst women has long been an accepted norm within American society; however, celibate males have unfortunately fallen outside of the scope of understanding for most. As a man, it was accepted (in fact encouraged) that I embrace my primal instincts and chase women with the end goal being sex. Sure, there are those who would bark about the double-standard that exists between men and women when it comes to sexuality, but at the surface of the issue, few would disagree with the prevailing wisdom that men are supposed to have sex – regardless of marital status. In fact, there was one instance in particular where I brought up my celibate journey with two male members of clergy in hopes of getting some sort of guidance or support and all I got in response was "good luck" and a handshake. *Are you kidding me?!*

And so, many of the women I would meet and date over the course of the months after Tasha would often fall into a similar pathology. They would be intrigued by my journey and acknowledge God's will for one's life, however, when it came to the brass-tax of the matter, they were uncomfortable with it. Uncomfortable because women are accustomed to being chased for sex and hardly encounter situations where this is not the case. For the women I dated, with this being the case, our interactions were oftentimes awkward and they would feel as though I didn't "care" about them or after some time would pass they would realize that they desired sex as much as those "dogs" they had dated in the past. That said, they would opt out of any further relationship with me as my lifestyle lacked a key component of what they had come to define as love.

This truth perplexed and frustrated me for some time. I can remember many nights feeling as though God had cursed me. Why me, I thought? As woman after woman did not pan out, I began to get discouraged. I started to believe that maybe the naysayers were right. Maybe God's commandments were a little dated and that in today's context, being in a monogamous relationship was the spiritual equivalent of being celibate in Bible days. Or so I thought. I tried every which way to convince myself that I would be ok to go back to living the way I had lived in the past. I would sometimes look to my friends and try to assess my life in comparison to theirs and doing so gave me the leverage I thought I needed to act outside of God's will for my life in this particular area. I was downright angry! I did not have a friend who was celibate and I had begun to lose faith in the belief that there would be a woman out there who would be willing to join me in the journey that God had assigned me to. I was ready to give up, but right at that moment-the moment when I was about to throw in the towel and concede to the desires of the flesh – God began a process of restoration in my life.

6

RESTORATION

Jeremiah 30:17 – "But I will restore you to health and heal your wounds,' declares the LORD, 'because you are called an outcast, Zion for whom no one cares."

$\mathscr{I}$ had reached a new low in my journey. All the times before that I felt despondent towards life, I knew that I was out of sync with God. But this time was much different. I felt that I was truly living out His will and yet, I still found myself frustrated and dejected about what the future held for me. It was in this broken state, that He began to do His majestic work. Unbeknownst to me, He had already placed my virtuous woman in my life long before my journey with Him even began. However, with Father like intuition, He knew that I would need to be in a humbled state to recognize the gift that He had for me. He had my best interest at heart and would prove Himself worthy of all praise in the months to follow.

But this time was much different. I felt that I was truly living out His will and yet, I still found myself frustrated and dejected about what the future held for me.

As 2007 came to a close, the Lord began to press upon my spirit an out of the box idea for celebration of the new year.

At this point, while my dating life had all but stalled, I had a pretty good routine going with daily indulgence in the Word and had really honed in on focusing my energy on seeking God's face. And so, God placed in my spirit that I should host a 24-hr fast at my home to bring in the new year. Now, this may not be an odd conviction to some, but just the year before I was host of a New Year's Eve party in Chicago that brought in about 300-400 people. Liquor flowed and girls scantily dressed draped the venue as me and my boys brought 2007 in with a bang. I share this not to brag, but to provide context around this request from God which was in stark contrast to how I had grown accustomed to spending my New Year's Eve's. Being that I was truly seeking Him at this point in my life and had come to a point that I was fully submitted, I yielded to this request.

Up until that point in my life, I had never participated in a physical fast. In the past I had "fasted" my cell phone, television and many other trivial things that distracted me from focusing on the things of God, but I had never once fasted food oddly enough. I suppose it was because I have always loved to eat. And I guess I never saw it as a true dependency or distraction away from God. Nonetheless, for this New Year's Eve celebration I was led by the Spirit to do a 24-hr absolute fast (no food or water). Now, as I've stated, I had never done anything like this before so I was somewhat intimidated by God's request of me. But, I did recognize the value that bringing in the new year with the Lord could have in my life and so I conceded to His will and began the planning for the event.

One of the first things I had to figure out was who to invite. Because of the purpose behind the event, I wanted to be very intentional with who to invite, as I wanted it to be an intimate setting where people who attended would not be precluded from freely worshipping God. With this in mind, I came up with a list of seven people to invite. These individuals were from various walks of life, most of whom I had become close to through our spiritual relatedness over the years. Aside from getting the attendees locked, I had to develop a program of sorts to guide us through our 24-hr journey. As such, I came up with an agenda that would call for praise and worship, deep scriptural study, prayer and lastly, reflection. It was a jammed packed agenda, but as I continued to work through the details of the event, I became more and more excited about what was to come. As I shared the agenda with the individuals I invited, their response was similar, although two eventually backed out. So, the final attendee list included Nneka, Kevin, Erin, Glen and Tina.

You may remember Nneka as part of my celibacy crew a few years back. Over the years, we had continued to build upon our friendship and she was someone I always considered serious about seeking God. Kevin and I were old college buddies. Ironically, we were never that close in college, however, one day while visiting campus on a recruiting trip we found ourselves engaged in a two hour long conversation about Christ. After that conversation, our mere acquaintance grew into a deep friendship as a result of our equal yoking. Erin was Kevin's girlfriend. She and I had met a time or two, but I had not had much of an opportunity to get to know her before. Nevertheless, I admired that she was willing to participate and follow Kevin's lead in the fast. In addition to Erin, Kevin brought Glen along as well. Glen, Kevin and I had spent a weekend together once during a T.D. Jakes conference and ever since, we always kept in touch with one another. I was very excited that Kevin had invited Glen because Glen was a minister and his depth of knowledge regarding the Word of God was well suited for our journey. Lastly, there was Tina. Tina and I had gone to school together. We had tried a time or two to date; however, it never really worked out. Nonetheless, Tina was someone with whom I had the opportunity to witness grow in Christ. She was on fire for the Lord and her presence was much welcomed for the event. So, in the end there were six of us, including myself, sitting in the living room of my house that evening, waiting on the clock to strike midnight, preparing to embark on a 24-hr spiritual journey with no specific destination in mind.

Looking back at it now, I can clearly see how God scripted the whole event. While Kevin and Erin were the only official couples in the room that evening, God had contrived a most masterful plan that would over time blow each and every one of our minds. Yes, there were three men and three women and while that orientation would appear convenient, I had never given it much thought. Even more ironically, up and till an hour before the event was to begin, I was not sure that Tina would make it and I was anticipating another one of my male friends to show up. But, that's not what God had planned and so, as the night unfolded God began to fuse spirits together in a way that would never be broken without our acknowledgement and by the time the fast had completed, His work was done.

We had a truly great time during the fast. Sure, there were moments where our flesh cried out for food and water, but in each moment of weakness we relied on the communion of one another and the Word of God. And though my mind at times could not quite comprehend how this would provide true sustenance, it did. As a result, we were sustained throughout the duration of the fast. Once the fast concluded, we embarked on a feast with all the trimmings. It was somewhat of a potluck and each one of us prepared some dish to quench our hunger. As we broke bread with one another and continued in deep fellowship, joy filled the room. Eventually, the time had come for us to part ways. And as we embraced one another and bid farewell, I reflected on the time we shared together and thanked the Lord for giving me an opportunity to be in position so that He could do His will.

However, not too long after the fast, I began to wallow in my own pity again. The source was once again related to women. I had reached a point of extreme frustration. I tried hard to embrace my singleness as a gift from God and was able to balance it pretty well, but when encountered with a female that struggled to accept me because of how "serious" I was about God, I found myself weary. I knew that God was testing my faith and I fought the desire to give up hard, but it had begun to weigh on me heavily each and every day. In an attempt to provide an outlet for my frustrations, I'd try to discuss them with Kevin, Nneka, even Jason or Will from time to time. But, no matter who I talked to, the sensation that I felt within would not go away. As customary with these types of dead-end moments in life, I found myself on my knees earnestly in prayer about my situation. Not only was I trying to pray my way out of the situation, but I also fasted periodically as well. I passionately wanted answers and found myself disappointed that I had let a situation truly steal my joy. This period of time for me was probably one of the most difficult to date and yet, I still clung to Jesus because I knew that the only way I would regain my peace would be through

Him. And then, almost within a blink of an eye, everything...
and I mean everything changed.

One day while on the phone talking to Nneka, I shared
with her these frustrations and my sense of lost peace. She
tried, as any friend would, to console me and even prayed with
me. She pointed to the things that God had already done for
me and the victories that had already been won. These points
were aimed at grounding me in the reality of the situation I
was dealing with. Though I had gotten past my frustration
with God per se (for leaving me in the single man's purgatory),
I still saw the possibility of finding a woman with whom I was
equally yoked and who would accept me for me, as highly
improbable. I had begun to lower my expectations and think
that my standards were too high. As Nneka listened to me
whine on and on, she firmly told me that it had to stop. She
explained to me that my behavior was not becoming of God.
That comment struck a chord within me. It was true that I was
down on myself, but never was it my intention to disappoint
God. I guess I had gotten so entrenched with my own thoughts
that I was unable to see the ungodliness of my ways. I thanked
Nneka for calling me out where I needed to be called out and
with that, we got off the phone because I knew I needed some
alone time with my Father.

I turned my cell phone on silent and knelt down at my
bedside to pray. As I prayed, thoughts of the type of woman I

wanted in my life were replaced with God's revelation of the characteristics of the woman He had specifically assigned to me. All of the characteristics that he outlined far exceeded my imagination. I was in awe of this mystery woman. And so, I sat there, on my knees waiting for God to tell me who she was and where she was. And then, He went silent. As I sat there for another few moments awaiting further revelation, none came. So, I concluded my prayer somewhat reluctantly and climbed into the bed. Unfortunately, I was unable to go right to sleep and as a result, I just stared at the ceiling. And then, just as the scales fell off Saul's eyes on the Damascus road, so did mine that night in my bed. The mystery was solved...I knew who this woman of God was that He had so vividly described. She had been in my life throughout each phase of my journey and yet I hadn't even realized it. But I was able to see clearly now. There she was, as beautiful as a dove, as meek as a fawn on a spring morning, my Proverbs 31 woman, my rib, the one He kept for me. Nneka.

> *God had done the heavy lifting, but it would be my job to take it across the finish line.*

Now that I had clarity on who she was, the big question was just how I was going to get her. I suppose the hard part was over. God had done the heavy lifting, but it would be my job to take it across the finish line. Though Nneka was my friend and we had known each other for years, I was very nervous about approaching her with a proposition to take our friendship to courtship. I was not even sure that Nneka felt the same way about me. And though I had God's sign-off, I wasn't sure that He had shared this revelation with her yet. That said, the situation had all the ingredients for a very embarrassing outcome. But, I had trusted God up to this point and I had already tried the dating scene on my own, so I was not too keen on going against Him on this one. And so, I devised a plan to get Nneka out on a date and once out I would tell her what God had placed on my heart.

Over the years, from time to time, Nneka and I would go and hangout. We would go check out movies or grab a bite to eat; just two friends catching up. Because this had some precedence, I decided to ask Nneka to meet me at a Dave and Buster's one Friday night so that we could "catch up." Though I thought she might have been a bit suspicious, she did not let on that she was aware that anything was going on. Before I knew it, the day had arrived. I was as nervous as I had ever been about anything in my life. I was confident in what God had revealed to me, but my flesh began to place doubts within me. *What if she did not feel "that" way about me? What if she is already "taken?"* Even with these doubts, I pressed on and went to Dave and Buster's to meet Nneka that Friday night in late March of 2008.

I arrived at Dave and Buster's before Nneka as she was running a little late. I suppose that was a good thing because it gave me an opportunity to gather myself before she arrived. About 15 minutes or so after I got there, Nneka arrived and made her way over to the booth where I was sitting. Over the next hour or so, we engaged in casual conversation, ate and genuinely just enjoyed one another's company. As I sat and listened to her share stories of things going on in and around her life, I found myself drifting off because I knew that there was still work to be done. We continued to converse for another 30 minutes or so and yet, I was still unable to find a convenient break in the conversation to bring up the "news." So, I decided for us to get up and go play some games to take the edge off. After we played two rounds of pool, I still had not broken the news to her. It was very frustrating and I began to feel that my time was slipping away. From pool, we went over to the bowling area/lounge and took a seat at the bar. We both ordered sodas and just continued to talk and then finally, I mustered up the courage to share with her what had been heavily weighing on my heart.

I shared my story with Nneka piece by piece. I recounted the frustrations I had been having with singleness. I told her that her friendship had really been a cornerstone in my life. Then, I broke into the heart of the matter. I told her I had been praying to God to send me a helpmate and that He had finally answered my prayer. *Her eyes widened.* I told her that it was her who God revealed to me. *Her face lit up with both shock and anxiety.* I continued on to share that while I did not know what the future held for us, I wanted to pursue a courtship with her. Ultimately, I wanted to allow God to have His will with our lives. *She sat, listening intently, with a subtle smile on her face.* As I concluded my monologue, there was a pleasant silence that existed before anyone spoke again. *I admired her beauty.* After a moment, she glanced down at her soda, took another sip and lifted her head back up in an angelic manner and began to speak. She told me that she too had been praying to God. *I exhaled a sigh of relief.* In fact, she had been praying to God about me. Wow. However, ironically, her prayers to Him were for Him to remove the emotions she had developed for me. *Ouch!* She told me that over the last six or so months, she had been fighting back emotions for me. One day she would like me and the next she would not; so much so that she had reached a point where she did not want to think about it anymore. As a result, my profession of love that evening was a complete surprise, albeit a pleasant one.

And just like that, we were a couple whose fate had been solely determined by God. I was ecstatic, as my nerves had finally calmed down, and knew that the future was bright for us. As we got up from the stools in the bowling area, Nneka reached out and grabbed my hand. The touch of her hand sent a warm sensation through my body that eventually produced a smile. I gazed back towards her direction and her eyes met mine with a sense of elation. We continued to stroll through Dave and Buster's, out into the parking lot, hands clasped and eyes firmly fixed on one another. Within a few minutes, we had finally reached our cars and we just stood there, holding hands looking at one another. A few more minutes passed by and we knew that we had to get going and so, we embraced one another and as we began to pull apart, stole a quick kiss to officially seal our status. I followed Nneka out of the parking lot that night to make sure she made it back to the highway safely. As she got outside of my view, I honked my horn and waved goodbye. As I continued on down the highway, I reflected on the night's events and caught myself smiling.

For the first time in my life, I knew what it meant to be in love.

It had been about three years since I had last been in a relationship with titles. And while that isn't a terribly long time, the fact of the matter is that within those two years, my now girlfriend was there the whole time. But, I am fully aware that everything happens for a reason and thus, the timing of Nneka and I getting together was truly God ordained. I would have never thought during our fast that New Year's eve that three months later she and I would have become an item. As a quick aside, remember Glen and Tina from the fast? Well, they too had become an item. Going into the fast there was only one relationship; however, three months after there were three. Think God had anything to do with that? Well, suffice it to say that we were all in amazement and He still had more in store for us.

My relationship with Nneka was beyond words. I had never met anyone so selfless, caring and understanding. To top it all off, she and I had become best friends. Sure, I still had my male compadres out there who were my "boys," but at this point in my life I spent the majority of my time either talking to or chilling with Nneka. Things were so good that in the first 8 or so months, we had not even argued. I was so unaccustomed to a drama-free relationship that I was truly beside myself. Additionally, as you might expect, we were living a celibate lifestyle and had committed to one another to follow God's commands as they related to sexual purity. However, in the beginning there were some interesting issues.

First off, we had a long distance relationship and as a result, we only saw each other during the weekends. Because of the distance, we had to spend the night at each other's houses (couldn't afford hotel stay that frequently). Now, I think it's obvious to see the challenges associated with this situation and during my first visit at her place, we were forced to face them head-on. As we were both preparing for bed that night, Nneka came into the living room and asked me if I was coming to bed. This question completely caught me off guard as I was sure she was just playing. But, as I looked at her face I could tell she was serious. As much as I wanted to oblige her, I had to decline and I told her that I would not be joining her. She was perplexed by my response because she didn't see what the issue was if we weren't going to do anything in the first place.

While the basis of her argument was rational, I had to explain to her that in the eyes of God, sleeping in the bed with her was unacceptable. No matter how innocent our intent, I knew that the bed was nothing more than a gateway to sex and I wasn't willing to risk our joint commitment to God on even my best intentions.

> *No matter how innocent our intent, I knew that the bed was nothing more than a gateway to sex and I wasn't willing to risk our joint commitment to God on even my best intentions.*

And so, she went back into her room and I eventually fell asleep on the air mattress. After that incident, the baseline was set and we did not have any other issues related to physical boundaries.

Another challenge that came up early on in our relationship was around affection. As a man, one who had only really given affection in the past as a bargaining chip for sex, I had a hard time adjusting to showing affection without being sexual. In fact, as a result of this issue, my default position was the complete absence of affection. Nneka called me out on this multiple times and expressed to me how it made her feel. While she understood that we were working to remain celibate, it didn't mean that I did not have to show affection. The lack of affection made her feel as if I was not interested (which I was!) and thus, made her question our relationship. As she shared this with me, it became obvious that I would have to adapt because my actions were impacting her. And so, through her patience and prayer, I was able to get to a point where I was able to show affection, a kiss on the cheek, holding of her hand, without being sexual. In all honesty, it was a refreshing change and I enjoyed the purity of the emotions expressed and received.

Though we had some challenges that we had to work through initially, my relationship with Nneka was growing exponentially each day. Our ability to work through these issues told me a lot about who she was and who we were as a couple. At any time, either one of us could have given up in frustration and deduced that doing it God's way wasn't feasible. But, neither of us did and we remained supportive and patient with each other and that is what allowed us to continue to have a fulfilling relationship; one that would carry us through the holiday season.

As the holidays approached, Nneka and I planned out how we would split them up. We decided that Thanksgiving would be held in Virginia and Christmas would be in Alabama.

By the end of the holidays, we had not only gotten to know each other more, but had a chance to spend time with each other's family. Just as important, both our families had a chance to spend time with us. Her mom and dad had really nice things to say about me and suggested coyly that things "must be serious if Nneka brought you home." As far as my parents were concerned, they spoke very highly of her after we returned from the holidays and seemed comforted that I was in a relationship with a "woman" for the first time. They loved that we shared the same spiritual convictions and worked together to keep God first. All in all, we couldn't have asked for a better holiday and we enjoyed every minute of it.

Sometime shortly after Christmas, I began to think more deeply about the future of our relationship. Things had been going so well and oftentimes when that is the case, we have a tendency to be adverse to change. But, at the same time, I recognized that Nneka was 29 going on 30 and that this age carried a ton of implications for women. Furthermore, God had already revealed Nneka and her purpose in my life to me. She was to be my wife. So, the big question that remained for me was, "what are you waiting for?" I could probably rattle off a thousand rationales for my hesitation, but I believe the most prevalent of them all was fear. I had no problem being in a "girlfriend/boyfriend, courtship" type of relationship. That was very familiar to me and still provided me with an "escape route." But, engagement meant a totally different thing and I was scared. As I entered 2009, I fought with this emotion daily. I knew that Nneka was the one for me, but I could not reconcile this truth with the deceptive voice within that kept telling me to wait. Wait on what, I was not sure.

Around the same time that I was fighting with "if or if not," I began to be plagued by what I like to call the "ghosts of sins past." As if toiling over what I was going to do as it related to my future with Nneka wasn't enough, I started to be bombarded by memories of sexual sins past; very vivid memories. It was almost as if I was going through some type of sexual detoxification and one by one, the women of my past would arise in my consciousness. Sometimes these "ghosts" would pop up at night as I fell asleep and other times, they would subconsciously show up in middle of the day. At one point, these "ghosts" were so persistent that it seemed they stayed with me throughout the day. I had never experienced anything like this. Sure, I had fantasized about women before, but never unintentionally. And what I found more troubling was the timing of these "ghosts." *Why now?* I was trying to make up my mind about whether or not I was going to propose to Nneka and now I had fight through these "ghosts" in order to think clearly. Somewhat bewildered by the whole thing, I reached out to Kevin and Jason to seek some prayer support. They both prayed with me and kept me on their nightly prayer list. In addition, they continued to check up on me from time to time to see how things were going. Through conversations with them and prayer, it became apparent that these "ghosts" and their timing were nothing but a ploy from the enemy to distract me and get me off track. In fact, their mere presence served as an affirmation of sorts that I was headed in the right direction. It was now clear that if I was going to get to an answer I was going to have to boldly press through challenges and continue to seek God's guidance and wisdom in the matter.

By the time mid-January came, my mind was completely consumed with this tug of war of when to move forward with my relationship with Nneka. As such, I sought out various counsel to get additional input into my decision-making process. One conversation in particular was with Pastor Lou. By the time Pastor Lou and I spoke, I had already begun the process of looking for an engagement ring just in case, but as I said earlier, I was still waiting for that "something" to push me over the edge. Pastor Lou was well aware of my relationship with Nneka. In fact, he used to be her manager and it was through her that he and I met. Over time, he and I developed a strong friendship and as a result, I had come to see him as somewhat of a spiritual mentor. And so, that afternoon when I called Pastor Lou to discuss the things on my heart, I had a feeling that he would be able to shed some light on the situation.

I opened up the conversation by telling Pastor Lou about how things were going and then went on to share with him that I had been going back and forth on the whole engagement piece. He responded by inquiring what my fear was and I shared with him that I did not know for certain. Part of me felt that the whole process had gone much faster than I had planned. Sure, I knew that God was in control, but I struggled to accept that with Him in control, things would not always go as I would have planned them. In a similar vein, Pastor Lou encouraged me to submit to God's will. He explained to me that part of my struggle was the result of me trying to pry the steering wheel back out of God's hand. He also shared with me in a jovial manner that it was a good thing that God is merciful, because if He had let go of the steering wheel when I wanted Him to, it is no telling what kind of chaos I would have caused. His words cut straight through to my heart and as a result, I found myself immensely convicted.

> Sure, I knew that God was in control, but I struggled to accept that with Him in control, things would not always go as I would have planned them.

As we were about to get off the phone, Pastor Lou asked me one last question. He asked me to explain to him why I would not move forward. Simply put, he said, "why not?" As I gathered my thoughts in response, I realized I did not have one. I did not truly have a reason not to move forward. He picked up on my lack of response and then proceeded to prod me for an explanation by suggesting different things. Did I not like the way she looked? Was she not domestic enough? Did she cause too much drama? Could I not see her being a good mother? He continued with a barrage of questions, but with each I responded with a simple answer of no. After hearing my final no response, Pastor Lou chuckled to himself and told me that if my answer to all of his questions was no then I was a lucky man. And with that, I received the final push that I needed to move forward. I did not have one real complaint about Nneka. After my conversation with Pastor Lou it became much more evident that this was the case. And so, when I got off the phone with him I quickly headed down to Jeweler's Row in Philadelphia and put a deposit down on the ring that I had been eyeing for a few months. My jeweler told me that it would take about two to three weeks to place the ring in the customized setting that I had requested. It was the most exciting day of my life and now I had to get ready to plan the proposal.

About a month or so leading up to the proposal, Nneka was really becoming frustrated with the whole "patiently waiting" thing. She wasn't the type to apply pressure, but I could tell by some of her statements that my ambiguity in regards to our future was becoming somewhat concerning to her. And sure, she was a faith all-star, but even stars can lose their radiance from the uncompromising roads of life sometimes. I say all of that to say that the week before the proposal, Nneka had conceded to not worry about if or when it would happen any longer. She had truly let go of the situation to allow God to be in control of this aspect of her life. Little did she know, what she had so longed for was right around the corner.

While it was hard for me to see her wrestle with this, it was great on the other hand because I knew that my proposal would be completely unexpected. Nneka had her own handbag business and one of the things she did as part of this venture was host handbag parties in various cities to showcase her latest handbag line. Well, April 18, 2009 was planned to be her spring/summer launch in Washington, D.C. I knew that I wanted to do something big for the proposal and I also wanted her friends to be around. As a result of the location of this particular handbag party, many of her closest friends were expected to be in attendance. With that knowledge, I eventually worked through the kinks of my plan with her best friend Porscha and was finally ready to pop the question!

The day had finally arrived and it was a hectic one because I had to conduct a workshop for parents in Philadelphia on how to talk to their kids about sex and the abstaining thereof. While hectic, it was very fulfilling and really set the tone for the entire day. Once I concluded my workshop, I headed down I-95 to DC to begin preparation for the big event. My first stop was Ruth's Chris Steakhouse because I had to meet with the manager to ensure that everything was a go. See, the catch was that the Ruth's Chris staff had to know that when "Porscha party of 15" arrived, that was code for my engagement party of 30 (I had invited an additional 15 people to share the moment with us). After meeting with the management and staff, I was assured that they were clear on the instructions and that they would not blow the surprise. After I left Ruth Chris, I went out to the National Harbor to check-in to the hotel. I had reserved a room with a nice view of the Potomac River (with separate sleeping quarters of course). After I checked into the hotel, I went ahead and prepared for the big event. While looking in the mirror and putting on the final touches of my ensemble, it began to hit me that I was about to receive the biggest and greatest gift that God had ever given me since His son Jesus. And so, with ring in hand (or in jacket pocket) I headed to the rendezvous point near the parking area outside Ruth's Chris to propose to the love of my life.

Around 9 pm Porscha called me and said that she and all of the friends from the handbag party were on their way to the restaurant. As such, I immediately texted the other people that I had invited and gave them a heads-up to get ready. Once inside the restaurant, Porscha made a toast to Nneka. Nneka thought this was kind of weird, but went along with the show. After the toast, Porscha blindfolded Nneka and then gave me a call again saying that it "was time." With that, I called all of the other guests again and told them to meet me in front of Ruth's Chris. When we arrived in front, Porscha came out and asked if I was ready and then went back in. Before heading in, I circled up with the other guests to say a quick prayer. It was a prayer of thanksgiving. All of the people in that circle recognized that without God, this momentous occasion would not have been possible. As I held the hand of the man next to me with my head bowed, my hands began to tremble. My nerves were starting to race. But before I could panic, I heard "Amen!" and with that everyone lifted their heads and looked towards me for acknowledgement that it was time to go inside.

We walked through the restaurant to the back room and when I was about 15 feet away I could see Nneka sitting there in the chair. She was as beautiful as I could have ever wanted my future fiancée to be on the night of our engagement. As we walked in the room, the other 15 guests that were already seated looked in bewilderment as to what was going on. Porscha had not shared with any of them what the occasion was as she didn't want to risk someone spoiling the surprise. For the most part, as soon as many of them saw me they put two and two together. I took a deep breath and walked in front of Nneka as she was seated and then stood facing towards her. Then Porscha said aloud "Are you ready?" And with that she removed the blindfold. No sooner than the blindfold was removed did Nneka begin sobbing tears of joy, for she quickly realized that her prayers had been answered. While she was crying, I grabbed her hand, leaned in towards her and asked her to stand. Once standing, I told her how thankful I was to God for placing her in my life. I told her how much I appreciated her for being her and how much I deeply and truly loved her. And then, I bent down on one knee and said that famed phrase known across the globe, "Will you marry me?" She said yes! And with that, we kissed and passionately embraced. As I stood there holding her, I found myself welling up inside as I began to reflect on God's grace and mercy. I thought about how I felt that His way was for the birds. I thought about all the things I had done wrong and how He loved me in spite of me. I thought about all the lonely days and nights when I cried out to Him for a helpmate. And just like that...my prayers had been answered. I had been restored. *God is good!*

7

TWO BECOME ONE

Genesis 2:24:"For this reason a man will leave his father and mother and be united to his wife, and they will become one flesh."

*O*ctober 17,2009. The weatherman is calling for cloudy skies with a chance of rain. Low 50's. That can't be good. I must admit, I'm pretty bummed about this. When I woke up this morning, I was sure this prediction would be wrong. After all, we've been fervent in prayer for it to be sunny and warm! *Surely, God, you can answer this simple prayer.*

I push back the curtains to peek out of the window on this early autumn morning. The conditions affirm the weatherman's forecast. *You've got to be kidding me.* I sit on the edge of bed, searching the sky for a break in the clouds and a sliver of sunshine somewhere. I can only imagine what must be running through Nneka's mind. For months I heard her talk about how she hoped for the perfect wedding day; how she dreamed of a day where the birds would sing gladly, the sun would shine brightly and the wind would be as still as a statue. As her husband-to-be, I want nothing more than to provide these things for her, but to my dismay, I can't. Weather conditions are outside of my scope of influence.

The time is now 8:34 a.m. Much of my present disappointments reside in the emotional toil that I know these clouds and mist are having on her. The day hasn't even begun yet. And of course, as part of the marriage tradition, I won't be able to check up on her. This is crazy. I want to speak to her. I just want to know how she's doing. *I know. I'll call on her the phone to do a pulse check.*

"Hey babe," I whisper.

"Hey baby," she replies. "How was the bachelor party? Did you have a good time bowling? Did you win?"

"Yea, it was cool. Didn't win though; had an off night I guess. My best score of the night was a 125. I think I was distracted, but I still had fun. How are you? You see the weather yet?"

"Well, that's good. At least you had fun. Yeah, I looked out the window a little earlier before you called. Kinda sucks, but it's cool. Nothing we can do about it, right?"

"Yea, you're right about that. Alright then, well, I'll let you go, but I just wanted to check on you to make sure you were doing alright."

"Awww...thanks babe."

"No problem! I love you."

"Love you too."

"Bye."

"Bye."

I hang up the phone and decide to lie down on the bed. I think I can steal just a few more minutes of sleep. Not surprisingly, I'm unsuccessful. My mind is racing a thousand miles per minute going over every detail of the day. I'm trying to sleep, but the significance of this day is finally sinking in. In less than ten hours, I'm going to be a *husband*. A husband.

I'm sure most would see this feat as a natural progression via the adult maturation process, but for me, this is so very different. Nothing could be further from the truth in my own life. Why? Because the journey that brought me to Nneka was a long, arduous and tumultuous one. One that, at many times along the way, I wanted to give up. One that, at many times along the way, I made mistakes from which I thought I would never recover. One that, at many times along the way, my own choices threatened to forfeit the very blessing that I sought to behold on this, my wedding day. Ironically, it was this same journey that shaped and molded me into the man that Nneka had come to love and trust enough to agree to become my bride. For that reason, I know that God's mighty hand is in all that is taking place right now. He knew exactly what I needed and He provided a woman for me that's just... just...beyond my wildest dreams.

The ceremony is set to begin at five thirty in the evening. Hopefully, the start time will prove beneficial as by early afternoon, much of the mist would have gone away and the clouds will become less dense. The day is so full of activity! It consists of me running here and there trying to complete the multitude of errands in preparation for my wedding night. And while I'm running all over the place from Petersburg to Chesterfield and back, Nneka is probably doing the same in Colonial Heights, placing the finishing touches on the reception décor, finishing up bouquets for her "inner circle" and doing what (I imagine) every bride does best: panic! Which by the way, let me tell you: instead of traditional bridesmaids and groomsmen, Nneka and I decided to create an "inner circle." This circle represents all of our friends throughout our lives who have played some role in shaping our character. This approach has allowed us to include everyone we love, as opposed to being limited to numbers via the bridesmaid and groomsman approach. But that's a side note. Back to Nneka. She's probably running around to get her nails done and if she is done with everything, I bet she's making that to-do list fuller than it needs to be.

I'm trying not to lose my cool, but I must admit: I'm becoming concerned. I think she's put too much on her plate. I think something will happen that will throw off her entire day. I've been calling and texting Porscha incessantly every hour on the hour. Thankfully, she's patient with me and she understands my concerns and the unquestionable nerves at work here.

It's 2pm. I pull up at Gillfield Baptist Church in Petersburg with my best men Wayne and Will in tow. Over the years, as an only child, I've grown to really value their friendships. They've become my true brothers. Wayne and I have known each other since around the age of seven or eight. We met during a "coach's pitch" baseball game in my hometown, Huntsville, AL. He was on the opposing team and as he tells it, I introduced myself to him, after reaching second base on a double, in an attempt to distract his attention in order to steal third base. While I don't agree with that version as it depicts me as a shady character, it cracks me up every time he tells it. So I've come to accept it as the truth. Ironically, not long after that baseball game, we ran into each other at my church. And it was here that our friendship began to take root and over the years we became inseparable. Though we didn't attend the same middle school, we did end up going to the same high school, arguably some of my most formative years. Wayne was my confidant during those high school years and days leading up to college. He was there when I first met Leann and every hurdle thereafter. He was the friend that kept a balanced perspective on everything and was very slow to judgment. This proved hugely beneficial as in those days I was somewhat easily frustrated and he was there more times than I can count to keep me grounded. Unfortunately, after high school we separated ways as we ended up at two different colleges a thousand or so miles apart. However, even with the distance, we kept in contact throughout the years and our friendship never wavered. It was this experience that served as an affirmation of sorts that Wayne would have to be here on my wedding day, as no one knew me better than him.

Will...well, you know Will already. He is my line brother and business partner with Theta Investments. For much of my young adult journey, he's been there for each and every twist, turn, up and down. Not only has he physically been there, but he's provided introspective counsel on many of the tough decisions I made along the way and as a result, in similar fashion with Wayne, there was no way I could have my wedding day without him present as my best man.

As soon as we enter the church, a familiar aroma hits me instantly. It had a somewhat nostalgic effect on me and immediately took me back to Union Hill Primitive Baptist Church in Huntsville, AL, where my spiritual development had begun. Though two different churches, the smells were surprisingly similar. I suppose it was God's way of acknowledging that I was in position to receive a blessing from Him. I suppose.

We walk down the hallway, which is lined with commercial tile and white brick walls. We're greeted by one of the deacons of the church. He instructs us to head to the pastor's conference room where we'll be able to hangout (i.e. stay out of the ladies' way) until the ceremony begins. When we walk into the conference room, I notice the various portraits on the wall depicting the lineage of pastors of the church. It's an awesome sight no doubt, but to my delight, it's also something to occupy my mind as the time continues to wind down.

We sit for a few minutes and before long, find ourselves reflecting on experiences of the past (the PG and church appropriate ones). Wayne recounts my adolescent years and Will enjoys teasing me about our young adult excursions. Laughter is flowing from one discussion to the next, and every 15 minutes or so, another member of my inner circle arrives. Before long, there are about sixteen of us in the conference room, breaking the proverbial bread with one another. I'm having a great time. This is a great experience. On one side of the room, two brothers are discussing the previous week's football games/scores and predicting the outcome of the games that Sunday. On the other end, you have three brothers in deep discussion about denominations of the Christian faith and spiritual disciplines. And not surprisingly, a few aloof brothers are in their own world, not engaged in any of the prevailing discussions, but texting away or halfway asleep. The atmosphere is very loose...just as I want it to be on my wedding day...a day of celebration.

It's now 3:30pm. My barber arrives thankfully (I was starting to get a bit nervous that he wasn't going to make it). As he strolls in, many of my friends give a very sarcastic look toward me. They can't believe that I had shipped my barber in for the big day. It's fine. I welcome their cynicism. It didn't matter much to me if they found this mighty vain of me. I knew how important this day was and as a result, I took every step possible to ensure that my bride would find me completely irresistible that evening. And so, he throws his cape over me and proceeds to tighten up my hairline to the humor of those looking on. He's finished after about 30 minutes and after he concludes, I head to the dressing room with Wayne to put on our tuxedos. Upon return to the conference room, I notice that the pastor has arrived. Time check: 415 pm. Only one hour and fifteen minutes before start time. I don't think I feel nervous, but my sweat glands are telling a different story. I can feel the perspiration through my shirt.

With my hands clasped together and elbows on my knees, I sit there and observe everyone in the room. Each of the men gathered around the table have played an integral role in getting me to this day. Some intentionally, some by default and others by chance. It didn't matter how it happened though. What mattered most for me was that it did happen and I was thankful it did.

I can't stop reflecting. I'm thinking on the experiences shared with each of them, and on the experiences to come. And in the midst of one of my thoughtful excursions, Pastor Lou interrupts us with a request for quorum. He begins speaking with us about the significance of the moment and how he excited he is to see us all there enjoying great fellowship with one another. Then, his attention shifts towards me. In a jovial manner, he asks about my mental state, as if to suggest that this moment was my last opportunity to get out. I burst into laughter. I feel pretty good. I suppose he's trying to lighten the mood with me.

So the room is now primed for intention. Jason speaks up and reads a few scriptures on God's purpose for and expectations of marriage. Jason had gotten married two years before and as a result, his words feel most appropriate and readily received. As we all sit in this room listening to what he's saying, the moment begins to grow right in front of me. He finishes what he wants to share, and then Kevin speaks up. Kevin decides to speak and touch on the roles of husband and wife. He's been married for about five months now, and so he's jokingly sharing the revelations revealed to him in those first few months of his marriage. When he finishes, a few of my single "inner circle" speak up and share their thoughts, concerns, etc. about marriage and the prospect of one day themselves getting married. The discussion is very thought provoking and calming. The look on everyone's face affirms that they too find this conversation valuable. Just as I begin to get comfortable as a spectator of this roundtable discussion, Pastor Lou interrupts again, but this time to let us know: "15 minutes until show time!" With that, we grab hands and he leads us in a prayer.

"If every voice and heart is clear, let's look to the Lord. Father God in heaven, we thank you today for the institution of marriage and we pray for your hand on this marriage ceremony and ultimately this marriage. We celebrate the things that you've already done in the lives of these two and we look forward to the blessings to come. We pray that you use today for your edification. It is in your son, Jesus name we pray...Amen."

I embrace each of the members of my inner circle, one by one. And with that, Pastor Lou, Wayne, Will and I exit the room to take our positions.

It's now 5:30pm, and as rehearsed, the ceremony begins with Stevie Wonder's "Ribbon in the Sky" as the prelude. As I peer through the doorway from the back hallway, I can see my parents begin their descent down the aisle. Wow. It's a very surreal moment for me because as my father and mother walk hand in hand, I realize that their leisurely stroll signifies the end of one journey and the beginning of another. They had taught me all they could from birth through adulthood. And though they would continue to be there for me, things would be forever different at the end of this day. My wife would now be my consoler, counselor, nurturer and all of the above. They would no longer be the first line of defense, but rather an option to be used sparingly in the years to come as I would begin to build with my wife.

Before long, they reach their seat and stand there as proud as I have ever seen them. My dad's poking out his chest and my mom's beauty is in full effect. I had no idea of the effect my marriage would have on them. As they sit down, it signals the cue for Pastor Lou, Will, Wayne and I to enter into the sanctuary.

We're now standing in front of the entire church, side by side. Pastor Lou is on the step above me and to my left are Wayne and Will. We all stand up straight, arms folded just below the waist with right hand over left. As I look out into the audience, I can't help but notice the flashes from the camera crew and pacing of the videographer. Their primary job is to make sure Nneka and I have the memories of this day forever. I try my best to avoid the camera's bright flashes, but I can't help it. I survey the room patiently to capture the familiar faces gathered here. People are here that have known me since birth, and some are here whom I have built relationships with since becoming an adult. For the most part, my entire life story can be told through the voices of those in attendance.

Across the aisle, on the right side of the sanctuary, Nneka's guests are seated and smiling. With expectant looks on their faces, I know they're awaiting the bride-to-be. I, of course, don't know all of them. Most of them I met throughout the time Nneka and I were dating. Still, I'm really glad to see them here. Nneka will be elated as well when she sees them.

I'm scanning the room. In comes Nneka's mother. Carrying the disposition of a proud parent, she gracefully walks down the aisle and takes her seat. After she enters, both of our inner circles make their way into the sanctuary from the side aisles. The men, dressed in black suits, white shirts and pink ties, file in one by one. They are definitely carrying a distinguished swagger, which compliments well what's occurring on the opposite side of the sanctuary. Black dresses, high heels, and pink bouquets in hand, the women elegantly walk stride by stride, harmoniously with the men, down the aisle toward the pews where they will all soon sit. Both groups reach their seats. All attention reverts to the center aisle. Nneka's younger sister enters first. *Like a princess.* She briskly makes her way down the aisle. *Must be uncomfortable with all this attention.* She takes her place, and then Porscha enters. Once Porscha reaches her position beside Ayanna, the ushers close the door. "Ribbon in the Sky" slowly fades away. The next song begins subtly in the background. The onlookers all stand in unison. And for a moment, in the transition of songs, all eyes were on me...or so it felt.

"The bride is coming, the bride is coming, the bride is coming," announces one of Nneka's four year old cousins.

"The one...I've waited for...my love's design. The one... He kept for me...until it was time," sings the soloist with pianist accompaniment. Nneka had picked this song about four or five months prior. She found it while scanning the internet and I vividly remember the smile on her face as she listened to it for the first time.

"Babe, I think this is the one! It's pretty much exactly how I feel about our coming together."

"Really? What's the name of it?" I inquired.

"The One He Kept For Me. It's by Maurette Brown Clark."

"Wow. The title alone says it all. I agree with you. It will be a great song for your entrance into the sanctuary."

As the soloist continues to sing, the double doors in the back of the sanctuary fling open and there she is – my beautiful bride. From head to toe, she's absolutely stunning. I mean, I already knew she was beautiful, but donned in her wedding dress, her beauty is taken to a whole new level that I had not before experienced. I can't stop grinning (and as some joked after the ceremony, I looked like a kid at Christmas).

I'm trying to keep my composure, but the way her beauty is radiating behind her translucent veil as she gracefully walks down the aisle in her father's arms, I just can't stop smiling. Luckily for me, at this point in the ceremony, no one is looking at me any more, as she is center stage, the main event. Once she gets to the end of the aisle, standing right in front of me, she and her dad halt their walk and await further instructions from Pastor Lou. As we all wait, I peek around the sanctuary and notice the smiles and tears of joy. It's an overwhelming feeling. Nneka and I lock eyes continually as we await the song to conclude. At various moments during the song, while standing there, Nneka gets a bit misty eyed and wipes her eyes in order to preserve her make-up. I have to admit: seeing my wife-to-be crying tears of joy is tough. I can feel the knot coming up in the back of my throat signifying tears to come, but I'm fighting hard to suppress them. I refuse to let myself breakdown in front of all of these people. Just as I realize that I'm beginning to lose the fight, the song concludes and Pastor Lou takes the mic, ultimately bailing me out.

After a brief introduction and welcome prayer, Pastor Lou kicks off the ceremony. The first order of business is for Nneka's father to hand over his beloved daughter to me.

"Who gives this woman to be wedded to this man today?" Pastor Lou exclaims.

"I do!" responds Nnekas's father and with that, he gives her a kiss on the cheek and hands her over to me. As I received her, we turn and face Pastor Lou, side by side, hands firmly clasped. While Pastor Lou works his way through his notebook, quoting scriptures and sharing jokes from our premarital sessions, Nneka and I are standing here in awe of one another. We squeeze each other's hand from time to time to express affection and when facing one another, we're winking and smiling at each other to get a reaction out of the other. In all honesty, we're having such great time that, shamefully, we don't really hear much of what Pastor Lou is saying (but, no worries, we have it on DVD to hear it over and over...and over again!).

It's like an eternity standing up here. But finally we reach the part of the ceremony that Nneka and I had long awaited for.

"Armond, do you take this woman whose right hand you now hold, to be your wedded wife, and do you promise before God and these witnesses that you will be to her a true and devoted husband; true to her in sickness and in health, in joy and in sorrow, in prosperity and in adversity; and that forsaking all others you will keep yourself to her, and to her only, until you are separated by death? If so, answer "I do."

"I do."

"Nneka,do you take this man whose right hand you now hold, to be your wedded husband, and do you promise before God and these witnesses that you will be to him a true and devoted wife; true to him in sickness and in health, in joy and in sorrow, in prosperity and in adversity; and that forsaking all others you will keep yourself to him, and to him only, until you are separated by death? If so, answer "I do."

"I do!" she says with a swerve of her hips to the surprise of everyone. The sanctuary erupts in laughter.

After Pastor Lou gathers himself from laughing, he concludes the ceremony by saying, "Therefore, by virtue of the authority vested in me as a minister of the Gospel of Jesus Christ, and in accordance with the will of God and the Sovereign State of Virginia, I now pronounce you husband and wife, one in name and one in faith. What God has joined together, let no man separate. Salute your bride!"

No sooner than the word "salute" exits his mouth, Nneka and I lock at the lips. We promised beforehand not to make a mess of each other while kissing and as such, after a few more succulent kisses, we turn to our family and friends, jump the ceremonial broom and walk toward the exit, waving happily to all in attendance.

We are now Mr. & Mrs. Mosley!

We are now Mr. & Mrs. Mosley!

We are now Mr. & Mrs. Mosley!

As we exit the sanctuary into a side area to await photos, we passionately embrace. Wow. I'm holding my wife, my beautiful bride. She's here in my arms. I can't help but think to myself, "Man, God is truly good!" It's only by His grace and mercy that I made it to this day. Though the journey itself was tumultuous at times, now that I have received the reward, I realize: every bump and bruise experienced had a divine purpose.

AFTERWORD
By Nneka H. Mosley

*G*rowing up, I always dreamed of one day getting married and having a family. I still remember my friend, Sonya and I, sitting on my aunts' steps in the 3rd grade talking about all the plans we had once we graduated from high school. I would end up attending Yale and she would be at Harvard. We would come out with great careers and end up married with a kid or two by 26. *Great life, right?* Well, as someone once said, "if you want to make God laugh, tell Him your plans." Clearly, that wasn't quite the plan He had for me.

I was a late bloomer in every aspect. I started everything "late" from growing breasts to having a boyfriend to losing my virginity. Like most high school kids, I wasn't very confident going in as a freshman. I hadn't had a boyfriend, never kissed a boy, let alone anything else with a boy. Actually I was quite a tomboy. Because of my thin stature at the time, I thought dressing in baggy jeans and big tops would mask the fact that I didn't have the womanly shape that some of my peers now had in high school which got the boys attention. As time went on, I ended up with my first real boyfriend in the 10th grade. He was a year older than me and definitely more "experienced." I guess you would consider it my first puppy love. He was so special that I even contemplated giving him my virginity. But I guess that wasn't in God's plan either because something always prevented it from happening.

After only 2 months, we broke up, and I was heartbroken. That was only the beginning of a long road of dating and heartbreak for me.

You know how some girls always have a boyfriend... well, I was definitely not one of them. I always managed to find guys to date, but it never lasted. Some could say that was partly my fault. True, I kind of knew that some of them were not worth my time before I got involved with them. Then there were those who completely pulled the wool over my eyes....had me thinking they were good guys when really they weren't. And of course, I can't forget those who really were good guys and showed interest in me that I had absolutely no interest in....go figure. I managed to get a little taste of guys across the spectrum during college and still somehow remained a "virgin" by most people's definition. Meaning I did everything but 'that' (actual intercourse). I guess a big part of it was that I always felt convicted whenever I participated in sexual acts. When I think back, almost every single time I was with a guy I would feel convicted before, during, after or all of the above when we engaged in sexual activities—even to the point of tears at times. Yet, I continued to do it. I think a part of me felt that since I wasn't going all the way, that made it a little better and maybe not as bad; which is probably one of the reasons

I kept doing it. Not to mention, I was always embarrassed to tell guys I was still a virgin for fear they would lose interest so I figured if I at least did some sexual things, it would hold their attention for a while. The worst they would think is that I was a 'tease.' *Lord I know I shouldn't be doing this, but at least I'm not having sex.* Or was I? In God's eyes, it was all wrong.

By the time I graduated from college, I had gotten to the point where I was "tired" of being a virgin. The Lord hadn't yet sent my Boaz or some great guy that could possibly be my husband, so why wait any longer? I was young and having fun, so why not? Not to mention, I was one of the only ones of my friends who still hadn't done "it" yet. So at age 22, I officially lost my virginity.

My early to mid twenties were interesting and fun. I was definitely a party girl. My friends and I didn't miss a beat. We traveled all over, partied, lived it up, and partied some more. During that time, I dealt with a number of guys. However, I was never lucky in the relationship department. I always wanted to be in a serious relationship, but nothing ever lasted. I remember praying to the Lord in the beginning of each one, asking Him to remove me from the situation if it wasn't for me....and every time, He answered and the relationship quickly came to an end. There were even times I didn't say that prayer because I really didn't want God to remove the guy out of my life. Yet, He still did. I never understood why I couldn't seem to meet and stay with a good guy. Was it me? Was I doing something wrong or sending out the wrong signals? Did I have a sign on my head saying, "Come talk to me if you are no good, a liar, not ready for a commitment, or full of drama?" I mean really! I still vividly remember nights and nights of crying myself to sleep because I just didn't understand why I was still single. Why was God doing this to me? I deserve to be happy too right? Needless to say, this was very frustrating to me especially when a number of my friends were in relationships.

The cycle of meeting a guy, developing feelings, having sex with him, and it not working out began to get really old. This was especially so since I already knew I shouldn't be having sex with them in the first place. Why do I keep doing this? During a few of my 'relationships,' I even tried talking to the guy about my spiritual convictions on having sex before marriage. And they actually agreed to us not having sex anymore, but it always ended up the same way. We would go without sex for awhile and eventually I'd always give in. And honestly, it wasn't always the guy initiating it. But I was always willing to give celibacy a try, but I knew I was never strong enough to stick with it if I didn't have a man who was on the same page.

By the time I turned 26, I had come out of my last short and unsuccessful relationship – one by the way I just knew would turn into marriage, and I was officially drained. At that point, I had determined in my mind that I would wait on who the Lord would send me because I was obviously not doing a good job picking men myself. For the next two and a half years, I remained single. And when I say single, I mean completely single. I kept in touch with a few guys from my past that I would see every so often, but that was about it. It never turned into anything and I definitely decided I would not be having sex any time soon. I wanted the next person I had sex with (if I had sex at all) to be the 'one.' Contrary to popular belief, something is NOT better than nothing. And I no longer wanted to waste time or exert energy with someone I knew there would be no future with just to have a guy around. I was so over giving away my goodies to men who in the end didn't deserve them. Now I know, the only person who truly deserved them was my husband. But you live and you learn.

Over the course of those particular years of singleness, I learned a lot about myself. I read a lot of books, prayed a lot and even fasted. I began to ask God to work on some things in me I needed help with. I also tried dating myself. For the first time in my life, I actually took myself to the movies. Not a big deal for a lot of people, but for some reason it was really refreshing to me. On April 1, 2006, I even penned a letter to my future husband. Obviously, I had no clue who he would be. I didn't tell anyone at the time, I just folded it up and tucked it away in my drawer with the hopes of one day giving it to my future fiancé before we got married. It read:

Dear Future Husband,

Although I don't know who you are right now, I want you to know I am praying for you each day. I know that the Lord is preparing us both, right at this very moment, so that when He brings us together we can be all He calls us to be as a union. I pray that both of our relationships with the Lord are rock solid so when we come together, no problem, difficulty, or circumstance will be able to tear us apart. I pray that you are a wonderful Godly man with noble character, a caring spirit, and a giving heart. I pray that we will always appreciate one another, respect one another, and never take each other for granted. I pray we will complement each other well and in being together, help one another become a better person. I envision us having fun with life and never forgetting laughter is the best medicine. I dream of us raising kids together and instilling in them Godly values. I hope that wherever you are and whatever you are going through right now is strengthening your faith and trust in God. I know God has a perfect plan for us both, so I am patiently waiting for the day we meet and/or come together. I don't even know who you are and I love you already. By the time you get to read this, we are going to be engaged! So, I thank you in advance for loving me unconditionally and I thank God for choosing me to be with you!

As I was writing that back then, I had no clue that two years later almost to the exact date of that letter, I'd enter into a relationship that would eventually turn into my marriage. Now don't get me wrong, I'm not trying to paint a picture like everything was just peachy during this time and patiently waiting was an easy thing to do because some days it wasn't. Despite learning to be content in the season I was in, I still had days when I felt somewhat hopeless. I still felt a little envious of others who were in relationships. I still sometimes questioned why God was taking so long to bring me a mate when others who seemingly weren't even remotely trying to live right had someone. Without realizing it, I think as Christians trying to live right we sometimes think *God is obligated* to bless us with what we want when we want it. Then we get sucked into the comparison game which is never a good thing because God has a different plan for each of us. I have definitely experienced this many a day and every time I have to remind myself not to go there. One thing God will teach you is patience...whether you want to accept the lesson or not. Nothing will happen before His appointed time. That's a fact. We all want our hearts desires now. And if that desire is in His will, it will come to pass, but sometimes we have to wait on it. I recognized that I was in a season of waiting and God was teaching me about the virtue of patience and trusting in His plan not my own. I had done it my way long enough and if I truly wanted the best God had for me, I had to give Him complete reign over it. So in my heart of hearts, I always knew the 'one' was on the way....just didn't know when he'd arrive and who he could possibly be?

While all this is going on, I managed to stay in touch with Armond, who I met back during an internship in college. Over the years, we grew close and developed a wonderful friendship. He was definitely what I considered a 'good guy' to be, just not for me. I remember always telling him, you are going to make someone a great husband one day! I laugh when I think back to that now. I mean, I even entered this man in one of those magazine searches for good men! I would actually try to think of people to hook him up with! We truly were just friends and I wanted him to be happy. And the thought of us getting together was, quite frankly, crazy to me at the time. But, God is funny. After years of just being friends, I suddenly found myself having thoughts of the possibility of us dating. I even remember thinking and laughing at how funny if would be if Armond ended up being my husband. A quick thought I found rather comical and one that would never come to pass in a million years. This is all when I seemingly had no interest in him whatsoever. So where was this coming from? I thought, maybe I am just lonely so I'm turning nothing into something. You know how us girls do sometimes. That had to be it right? Or maybe despite the fact that he wasn't my usual "type," wasn't older than me, and wasn't exactly who I envisioned I would end up with, God was slowly positioning me to appreciate all that he was. He was God fearing, trustworthy, compassionate, and smart. He was a man of his word, respectful, encouraging, disciplined, and family oriented. He was the type of man I wrote about in my letter and he was right in front of my face for the past 7 years. I always recognized those characteristics, but not in terms for me. But, God's timing is never off and I realized that maybe the reason we never looked at each other as potential love interest before is because God was preparing us both at the same time to be in a position to come together. If either of us had forced it any sooner, perhaps we wouldn't be where we are today. We each had to go through some things, grow, be broken, and rely completely on the Lord before He united us together.

I share this with you all to especially say to my single sisters to stay encouraged. I know it sounds cliché...you hear it all the time. And Lord knows I remember the frustration of being single only to have some married woman tell me to stay encouraged while she gets to go home to her husband and I'm sitting at home alone every night. What in the world could she possibly know about what I'm feeling...she has a man! But, before you roll your eyes up in the back of your head, hear me out. I do know the feeling. Being single was something I didn't always handle well. I had been involved in some form of sexual sin since I was 15 and the root of it all was me trying to appease a man. Trying to do what I could to get and keep a man and not be single. To think how many times I have put a man and my own desires over my relationship with the Lord is pathetic to me. The more I did it, the more convicted and disconnected from God I felt. Sexual sin and any other sin draws us away from God and the deeper we go in sin, the harder it is to climb out.

Although I always had a desire to be with a God-fearing man who would be okay with not having sex before marriage, I honestly didn't think I would ever find one. But it was never my job to find him any way. I had to give that to God and trust that in His perfect timing, He would bring me who He wanted for me. If I believed in God's Word, I had to trust that no matter how long it seemed to be taking, what was in His will would come to pass. Waiting on anything is never fun especially when you want it right now. But looking back, I'm grateful that the Lord allowed me to go through some of the things I did. It made me appreciate even more the gift He blessed me with in having Armond as a husband. In the end, all the nights of loneliness, tears, and heartache were worth it.

This book is not just a story about a man and how he came to meet his wife. It is a story of growth, patience, trusting in God's plan, repentance, and restoration. This doesn't just apply to sexual sin, relationships or finding a mate, it can apply to any area of your life. It's a daily walk trying to live right. None of us will ever be perfect. We will mess up sometimes, but thank God he doesn't leave us hanging when we do. We get a new chance each day we wake up to try again... *"forgetting what lies behind straining forward to what lies ahead!"*[1]

---

1   Philippians 3:13

STATEMENT OF REDEDICATION

I,_____, rededicate myself to Christ today, _____ _____, 20_____. I confess that I have allowed sexual sin to have dominion over my life and thus, created an environment that has served to disconnect me from God the Father. In full humility, I now repent and ask for forgiveness in Jesus' name. From this day forward, I promise to work each day to turn away the sexual desires of my flesh and pursue a life that is "holy and acceptable to God."[1] I acknowledge that I am not perfect and believe that the journey towards restoration can only be found in the strength given unto me by Jesus Christ. It is my prayer that He sustain and keep me each day in my walk of rededication.

---

[1]   Romans 12:1

THE *Redediction* WORKBOOK

INTRODUCTION

"Nobody can go back and start a new beginning, but anyone can start today and make a new ending." – Maria Robinson

Change is one of the hardest things to do. By completing and signing the statement of rededication, you have said that you are ready for change in your life. In repentantly acknowledging that sexual sin has held you captive in the past, you have now opened yourself up to God for his redemptive and restorative work to take place in your life. In many respects, the hard work is done because you have turned things over to God and put your trust in Him. However, there is still work to be done. As you prepare to embark on your own journey of rededication in search of restoration, remember that it is a process. If your journey is anything like mine, you will have some good days and bad days. You will experience the favor of the Lord and at other times, you'll feel a cold chill from His perceived absence. You will meet some awesome new people, but you may also grieve the loss of old friends. You will establish refreshing new habits and you will find yourself exhausted from fighting temptations of the past. Many of these struggles will be welcomed as part of sanctification, but others will frustrate you because they'll appear uncalled for. *God, is all that really necessary?* But, no matter what challenges may come, know that because of your renewed faithfulness, God has now taken you by His hands and will begin to shape and mold you into a new and better you! You will find this new you to be the youyou always knew existed within, but were unsure of how to set him/her free. And now that you are free, God will call you to new places in life in order to take part in the fulfillment of His will. Get ready for Him to do exceeding and abundantly above all things that you can ask or think![1]

I'm so excited that you have decided to hand over the sexual sin to Christ and have committed to the pursuit of celibacy until marriage. Know this: the enemy is not happy with this decision. In fact, he is now going to work even harder than he did in the past to get you to give up hope and to convince you to turn away from God. But, also take comfort in knowing that you are not alone. With God re-established at the center of your life, you have all that you need in order to be victorious. His grace is sufficient[2] and I implore you to lean on Him and not your own understanding in time of tribulation. That said, my prayer is that the following pages equip you with the knowledge and methods necessary to augment the

---

1   Ephesians 3:20
2   Corinthians 12:9

process that God has already begun. As I said earlier, it is a process so, sit back, get your pen and paper out and prepare for a life changing journey!

PHASE I: PURGING

[Purging (verb)– to make free of something unwanted]

*P*hase I of the celibate journey is called Purging. As someone who has recently decided to commit to celibacy until marriage, purging will be critical in order to move forward in the process. By purging, I mean the removal of things in your life that can serve to hinder you from maintaining this commitment. These things can be any of the following:

1. Memories
2. Relationships
3. Friendships
4. Known Vices

While the four things above do not represent all of the potential "things" that might stand in the way of your pursuit of God's will, they do represent a large majority of the things that I found problematic in my own walk. Let's take a look at each one, one by one.

Memories

Around the time that I was wrestling with the decision to get engaged or not, I was bombarded with what I call "ghosts of sins past." These "ghosts" represented the memories of each and every sexual encounter in my life. Though I was not consciously trying to recall them, I found myself being haunted by these "ghosts" or memories for quite some time. In reflecting on what happened, I now know that the reason these "ghosts" caught me off-guard and began taunting me, in the face of a critical decision point in my life, was because I had not dealt with them in the earlier stages of my journey. Honestly, it was a shameful time period because I felt as though I was cheating on my soon-to-be fiancé because of the frequency in which these memories came to mind. One by one, each sexual experience replayed itself internally and I was tormented. I did not know what to do and ultimately, I was embarrassed.

You must confront the sins of your past and the memories of your wayward years forthrightly. I did not do this. Instead, I tried to dance around the "pink elephant" in the room as if it wasn't there. Part of the confrontation process is the genuine repenting for each sin committed. In the initial phases of my journey, I spent a lot of time focused on being celibate as opposed to introspective repentance. By introspective repentance, I mean the process of sitting and reflecting on the sins of the past and placing each one on the altar in order for the blood of Jesus to cover them. Sure, I had asked God for forgiveness, but I did so in the aggregate sense and as a result, I avoided the challenge of boldly confronting my past. As a result, I left myself open to those "ghosts" I spoke of later in my journey; in times where I was most vulnerable. This could have been detrimental to me, but thankfully God covered me and protected me from my own self in order for my commitment to remain firm.

Moment of Introspection:

- *What memories do you need purged in order to move*
  forward with your celibate walk?

ACTION: As you recall the memories, write them down on a sheet of paper. Once you have them written down, go to the Lord in prayer and seek His forgiveness. After you have prayed, rip this sheet of paper up and throw it away to symbolize the complete purging away of these memories from your life.

RELATIONSHIPS

"People come into your life for a reason, a season or a lifetime."[1] This timeless quotation is so simple, yet so profound. One of the harder parts of change is the transition of relationships. The harsh reality of the journey that you've embarked upon is that there will be relationships that you will have to leave behind, or purge. **Every relationship that you have today is not beneficial for your tomorrow.**

The relationship piece really breaks down into two subcategories. The first relates to male-female relationships (boyfriend/girlfriend). You may be in a relationship with someone today. You and that person have probably enjoyed some great memories together and then, one day, you informed them that you were going to give this "God thing" a chance and become celibate. If your significant other is anything like mine was in the past, I'm sure they probably received this message with some level of shock and surprise. Many, after the initial response, will come around and accept this proclamation. Others however, will poke and prod and persist in their attempts to second guess your decision. While their second guessing may not be of malicious intent, at this phase of your journey their questioning only provides an obstacle for you to overcome; one that may be too steep to climb. You're probably thinking to yourself right now that ending

---

1   Author Unknown

a relationship with a boyfriend/girlfriend on the grounds of misalignment on the issue of celibacy is a bit extreme. I completely understand. However, I would submit to you that continuing in a relationship in which your commitment to celibacy is not understood and/or respected will only serve to pose significant problems as you prepare to take-off.

Can you change their mind? As noble as it may seem, this is not the best evangelistic moment because you probably have not quite figured the whole celibacy thing out yet. Why are you celibate? What does it mean? What is permissible? What is not? These are things that I pray you come to understand in the days to follow, but, if you're anything like me, you probably do not know yet. Not surprisingly, my naïveté put me at unnecessary risk before even getting started good. For example, initially I thought "everything but sexual intercourse" is what celibacy meant. An obvious misunderstanding (and an embarrassing one at that), but one that served to keep me steeped in sin for much of the beginning of my celibate walk. Now, at the time, my girlfriend understood and respected the journey. However, as a result of my misunderstanding, I sent her a ton of mixed messages through my actions which ultimately made her skeptical of the walk as a whole. See the damage that misunderstanding can cause? How much more would it cause in a relationship with a person that does not understand or respect the journey? **The risk is not just**

limited to you, but to the other person involved as well.

So, if you're in a relationship with someone and they understand and respect your journey, great! You don't have to end it, but be ever so mindful of the issues that your misunderstandings can have on them. In order to mitigate this, you will need to tread softly on trying to educate them until you yourself are first fully educated (we'll focus on how to achieve this in Phase II). Consequently, this approach may pose challenges as your decision will be sure to bring questions. But, if you want to remain in the relationship, you must ask your significant other to be patient with you in order to allow the situation to become clearer over time.

If you're in a relationship with someone and they do not understand or respect your journey, please end it immediately. Is there a chance that it might work out in your favor? Sure. But, I've seen this situation go sour too many times to believe its happenstance. **What's even more critical to this issue is that your pledge of celibacy is about God first, you second.** Trying to wait it out for a significant other would be putting yourself in front of God and that does not resemble someone who has submitted themselves to God and His commands. Ultimately, if you want to get what God has for you and not just what you can see, there will be some trust required during this journey. And what better place to start than here?

MOMENT OF INTROSPECTION:

- *How do you think your boyfriend/girlfriend will respond to your pursuit of celibacy?*

ACTION: Before speaking with them, be sure to think through what you want to say. Remember, this revelation is yours and it is important that you bring it to them in a loving manner. Avoid any "holier than thou" talk. While it is ultimately up to them to receive your message, how you package it is extremely important.

- *Do you trust that whatever the outcome of your relationship, God has your back? Why or Why not?*

FRIENDSHIPS

The second subcategory of relationships is that of friends. As the quote suggests in the beginning of this section, people will enter into your life at different points and for different purposes. With friends, we see this truth even more clearly as they come and go more frequently and are more varied over the course of our lives. Of course, you probably can count on two hands the number of true friends you have at this point in your life and the remainder would probably fall into the acquaintance bucket. An interesting thing about this journey is that it may require the demotion of some of those friends and the promotion of some of your acquaintances.

In contrast to the boyfriend/girlfriend relationship, friends are typically more tolerable to change. They usually aren't as directly impacted and can most times keep moving with their other friends without missing a beat. As such, there may be friendships that you recognize as non-beneficial to your walk that can linger on in the absence of any direct confrontation. But, lingering is not a good thing. For example, before I began my journey, I had amassed quite a few friends in my life. I was never short on having someone to go out with to the clubs or any other spiritually inconsistent adventure. Interestingly enough, as I began to walk with the Lord on the celibacy journey for awhile, I began to see that many of these relationships werecounterproductive to what I was trying to accomplish. Why? Because they were still participating in the very same activities that I had laid at the altar just a few weeks ago. However, I hesitated to end them and at the most inopportune times they would seek me out to re-engage in the behaviors of the past. Friends are influential and keeping certain friends around (who are still reveling in the same sin area that you are trying to escape), is dangerous. No matter how good intentioned he may be, it would be silly for a newly recovering drug addict to go back into the environment in which he once enjoyed those substances. In similar fashion, you're only fooling yourself if you think that you can keep up the same level of intensity with the friends who continue to do the things you have now turned away from. And so, it is key that you don't conveniently avoid addressing the relationships you have with people who unknowingly have a great potential of dragging you back into the past.

Am I saying that you have to cut your friends off completely? No, not at all. But, what I am saying is that through the process of purging, there will be some pruning necessary as it relates to your friends. In the early stages of my walk, I experienced some isolation as many of my friends were weaned off by my new lifestyle. They no longer felt comfortable telling me the stories about the girls they slept with and I no longer felt comfortable hearing them. For those friends that were true friends, over time we were able to rebuild our friendship on mutual respect that did not cross those lines. For those others, we still today maintain a rather "touch and go" friendship. There are no hard feelings, but just an unspoken acknowledgement that a change has occurred. As you begin this journey, you must be aware that following Jesus comes at a cost. In my experience, some of my friends were this cost. And though it may initially hurt, I promise you that God will restore everything you feel you may have lost and then some!

MOMENT OF INTROSPECTION:

- *Who are your closest friends today?*

ACTION: Create a list of all of your friends. Beside each friend, describe what you most value about that friend. Review this list and pray that God provide you discernment regarding your friendships.

- *How will your friends react to your journey?*

- *Do you have any acquaintances that you think should be promoted to friends as a result of your journey?*

- *Are you willing to forfeit friendships in order to pursue God's command? If not, why not?*

KNOWN VICES

What is it that gets you riled up sexually? What are the vices that serve to create the environment or inputs that ultimately result in your pursuit of sex and all things considered sexual? For me, I found alcohol and clubs to be at the top of my list. These two things together almost always put me in the mood for sex or the pursuit thereof. As I began my celibate journey, I knew that I would have to purge myself of my known vices if I were going to have a fighting chance at maintaining my commitment to God. If you recall, during my first 40-day stint of celibacy, I also gave up music and television in addition to alcohol and clubs. The reason I did this is because at the time I was aware of the influence that each had on me. While alcohol and clubs had a much more pervasive effect, each of them individually were responsible for adding some amount of fuel to the proverbial fire in my loins.

As part of the purging process, it is critical that you remove the known vices from your life. Most likely, you already know what they are. Unfortunately, no one can tell you what these are for you. Alcohol and clubs may not be vices for you and as a result, don't serve as enablers for your sexual desires. Maybe. You may suffer from pornography. Or maybe it's having company past a certain time of night. Whatever the vices are, before you get going with the journey it is of the utmost importance that you identify them and begin to purge them from your life. Some will be easier to remove than others, but don't get discouraged by how challenging they might at first appear. **Remember, you are undergoing a process and God will be with you every step of the way.** In similar fashion with memories, you will need to take each of these vices to God in prayer and seek His strength in order to successfully abstain from them. Once you've done this, you will need to practice some discipline and begin the daily process of denying self[1] in order to more fully pursue God's will for your life. Some days you'll get an A and others you'll get a D. Try not to keep track of the wins and losses, but focus on the process of restoration that has begun. As the saying goes, "Rome wasn't built in a day," and neither will the new you. Many of these vices have been with you since adolescence, so be patient with their exit (but...not too patient!). What is most important is that you trudge forward each day, continually striving to keep God's command of purity.

While we've spent some time discussing the known vices, be aware that there are probably a few unknown vices that exist as well. These will be revealed as you progress along your journey. Don't be alarmed by them when they arise, but be thankful that they have moved from the dark places in your life into the light. Their now conscious existence is reason

---

1   Matthew 16:24

for joy because they serve to affirm growth! Use this sign of growth as a source of encouragement to continue to press forward. You are on the right track! And don't worry; there will be many more moments like this along the way.

MOMENT OF INTROSPECTION:

- *What are your known vices?*

ACTION: Write down your known vices. Beside each one, answer the following questions:

- *If sex were not an option, would I still engage in this? Explain your answer.*

- *What is the source of this vice? Personal preference? Peer pressure? Parents or upbringing? Explain your answer.*

Most likely, as you work your way through the process of purging, you'll feel some internal (and possibly external) resistance. You will find yourself trying to hold on to certain things and people along the way. The more you resist and refuse to relinquish your full self to God, the more frustrating this reality will become. For some things, purging will occur organically, and for others, your concerted effort will be required. As you press through the frustration, you will ultimately reach a point where you feel isolated and lonely. When you reach this point, you will know that purging has taken place. Though there may still be things internally and externally that need purging, enough of the "stuff" that served to block you from seeing and hearing God clearly in the past will have now been removed. And so, now you sit…in the quiet calm of the Lord. It is in this desolation that phase II can begin. God will begin to fill the voids left behind by the memories of the past, relationships of old, outgrown friendships and known vices. He will begin to nourish you with the Word and through the Spirit. *Nourishing* is where the scales of life will begin to fall off[1] and you will be strengthened and prepared to walk boldly in your new, rededicated life; a life absent of sexual immorality.

---

[1]   Acts 9:18

PHASE II: NOURISHING

[Nourishing (verb)– to promote the growth of]

To me, Nourishing is the most exciting phase of the process of restoration. **Where Purging focused a lot on the past, *Nourishing* will focus on the present in preparation for the future.** One of the biggest missteps I made in the initial days of my walk was that I did not take the time to feed my spiritual self. For some reason, I thought that just hearing God speak and convict me on the issue of sexual sin was enough. I had heard many a sermon on sexual sin and it not being God's will, but honestly, I had never really searched the scriptures for myself. As "luck" would have it, my ignorance led to much misunderstanding (and embarrassment). Phase II of the journey is the most critical piece to enable you to move from repentance to restoration. There is no activity more important than nourishing in this journey because without it you will lack the fortitude required to sustain the attacks of the enemy. Given the vulnerability created by purging oneself, the process of nourishing will help to cover and strengthen you. In effect, there are really three parts to *Nourishing* and they are as follows:

1. Connection with Local Church
2. Studying the Word
3. Developing a Prayer Life

While these three do not have to be done in the order listed, it is important that you focus on addressing these three areas as part of your nourishment process. In fact, at the end of Phase II, you will come to realize that these three are interrelated and a healthy balance is required for each to be individually effective.

CONNECTION WITH LOCAL CHURCH

There was a point in my life where I proclaimed that I was spiritual, not religious. Why? Because I had come to a point in my early young adult life where I struggled to see the benefit of organized religion; namely church. Truth be told, the main point of consternation for me was the inconvenience that its "required" attendance presented on my less than pious lifestyle. At the end of the day, I felt that church just was not required for my relationship with Christ. Sure, I was aware of the scripture that states to not forsake the assembly[1], but I did not pay it too much attention. And all the while I was fighting the church, I never realized its value and how it might have helped to spur me back towards the Lord much sooner.

You may be like I was. You might be one who considers themselves spiritual, not religious. If so, I get it. I understand this position, but let me suggest to you that now, as part of your rededication and pursuit of living a more holy life, you give the church another try. As I recount my own journey, it wasn't until I had fully connected back with the church that God began to press me hard and reveal His will for my life. Outside of the church I had received glimpses of His will and heard bits and pieces, but it wasn't until I joined a church and became active again, that He fully revealed His purpose to

---

1   Hebrews 10:25

me. And for this reason, I recommend that you connect with a local church.

The fact that you're reading this part of the book means that God has already begun a work in you. He's called you out of sexual sin. But, that's not where the journey ends. Our God is a big God and His plans for our lives are much greater than we can imagine. There are things and people that He wants to connect you to that can only be brought forth through your connection with His church. For example, in the church, there may be a young man or woman who is in the very place you are in today. They are seeking a way out of sexual sin and need encouragement to begin the journey. How much could you help this person given your current situation? Or, maybe there is someone in the church who has recently gotten married, but remained celibate until they exchanged their vows. Would that not be a great connection for you? Could you find these types of people outside of the church? It's possible, but the key difference is that beginning with the church establishes a baseline that is essential; Jesus is Lord and Savior. A lot of people do a lot of things for various reasons, but in this walk you need to be sure you are connected with people of a similar mindset as it relates to the Lord. He is your sustainer and without a mutual understanding of Him, you could easily find yourself too trusting in another individual and ultimately hurt.

If you are currently part of a local church, my question to you would be around your level of activity. Connectedness goes beyond membership and thus, part of what is required in order to unlock the power of connection with the church is participation. Participation is a key differentiator for the experience that people have with the church. When you look at the process of *Nourishing*, a key component that enables or promotes growth is engagement. While you will meet some people by happenstance, as you look to nourish yourself you will need to step out of your comfort zone and meet new people. In meeting new people you will expose yourself to growth because not everyone thinks and feels the same way you do about Christ. Through participation and activity, you make yourself available to be taught as well as to teach. After all, your story isn't yours to keep to yourself. Someone needs to hear it and how will they do that if you are not in a position to share. This process of being taught and teaching is in line with the scripture that suggests *iron sharpens iron*[1]. So, as you can see, church connection by way of membership and participation will afford you the foundations of growth in order to catapult you into the next component of *Nourishing*.

---

1   Proverbs 27:17

MOMENT OF INTROSPECTION:

- *Are you connected with a local church? If not, why not? If so, are you active?*

ACTION: Research ministry opportunities within your local church (if you are already a member) or a local church (if you are seeking a church home). Identify three that interest you. Write down a sentence or two about why these ministries in particular interest you. Pray to God on these ministry opportunities.

- *Do you have a testimony? If so, what is it?*

ACTION: Write out your testimony and store it somewhere safe for future retrieval. Note: You may have more than one.

- *In what setting would you be most comfortable sharing your testimony? Why?*

STUDYING THE WORD

Now that you have reconnected with the church, the next part of *Nourishing* is studying the Word. I admit, at first glance, this component may seem to be cliché. From the beginning of time it seems, I can remember the elders of the church instructing us as babes in Christ to study the Word. No matter how emphatic or persuasive this message was shared with me, it never gained much traction until I sincerely committed myself to God and reconnected with the church. There were plenty of days during high school, college and after where I'd read the Word, but over the years I've learned that studying the Word is much different. To study the Word is to get past the platitudes of God and really begin to dig into what He has to say about the more concerning issues of the heart. You know the platitudes right? They are those phrases that we throw around casually in hopes that we inspire ourselves and maybe even someone else. *God is good! I'm blessed and highly favored!* Though these declarations are true, they do not require an in depth study of the Word to conclude. Furthermore, they have the potential to allow us to remain stagnant because they have an external focus on God, in that which He has done or will do for us. The Word has the uncanny ability to cause change[1] and it is change that you are now looking for in this phase of your journey.

---

[1]   2 Timothy 3:16–17

Aside from the Word's ability to change, studying it is also critical for understanding the very journey that you're on. All too often we subscribe to ways of living per the Word, but have not done the study required to fully justify our actions[1]. Sure, grace will abound[2], but it is imperative in this journey that you become familiar with what the Word says about sexual immorality. Part of the confusion I had during the beginning of my celibate walk was related to my ambiguous understanding of God's command of sexual purity. Growing up, I always heard my Pastor and other pulpit staff speak of not having sex. As a teenager, I internalized this to mean that God's will was that I did not engage in sexual intercourse. This understanding was simple enough to process. After all, you did not get kudos from friends for doing anything else; all that mattered was whether or not penetration occurred. And so, I lived most of my life with this perverted reality of what God really meant regarding this area of my life. But, if I would have searched the scriptures for myself and studied them, I would have come to a more complete understanding of God's intention (See the Appendix "Why Celibacy" for a full bible study on this.).

So, how do you study? Well, for me it began with picking out a time of day that I knew would not conflict so that I could develop the habit of studying. Part of the challenge

1   2 Timothy 3:15
2   2Corinthians 9:8

with studying the Word is consistency. We've all done it; made these grandiose commitments to read the bible in its entirety in a year and before we finish week 1, we find ourselves two or three days behind. If we're resilient, we may try again only to find ourselves back in the same position a few weeks later. And then, as life would have it, we subconsciously give up. Trust me, I've been there! To change this pattern you will have to pick out a specific time of day. I found early mornings to work best for me because the only excuse I would have if I did not study would be my own laziness. Though mornings worked well for a period of time, I have had to adjust my study time here and there to fit certain life changes. A key part of the scheduling is to be flexibly disciplined. It is ok to change your time with the Word if it no longer works based on your schedule. The worst thing you can do is to try to force fit it in and ultimately, you'll end up not studying and extremely frustrated.

With your time locked, it's now time to begin studying. But where, you might be asking yourself. Great question. Depending on who you ask, you'll get a wide variety of responses as to the starting point of any good study curriculum. For the purposes of the journey that you are on, I recommend that you begin in 1 Corinthians, with a specific focus on Chapter 6. Please read the entire book to grasp the full context (if you don't have a "Study Bible," I suggest you purchase one as they are an invaluable resource as you begin to dig into God's Word.). From 1 Corinthians, I would next go to Colossians, focusing particularly on Chapter 3, and then, to Romans and do a deep dive on Chapter 12. In my opinion, these are some great starting points as it relates to gaining an understanding of God's command regarding sexual purity. In addition, these books of the Bible are rich in content and I am positive that they will lead you to other places in the Bible as your spiritual appetite is awakened. Be sure to take notes as you read because you will have questions and need to revisit them later with clergy in your church (see how being connected to a church ties back in?!). Studying the Word is not easy by any stretch of the imagination, but with discipline you will give yourself the opportunity for the Holy Spirit to work in you to teach and clarify as you study. As you study, keep an open mind. Sure the journey began with celibacy, but there's no telling where God wants to take you as He nourishes you with the Word. Be prepared for a life changing experience!

MOMENT OF INTROSPECTION:

- *How often do you study the Word?*

ACTION: Pick a time of day that will work for you to study the Word every day. On a calendar, count out 30 days from today and mark day 30. Commit to studying the Word at your designated time each day for 30 straight days. A mentor once told me that if you do something for 30 days it becomes a habit.

- *Besides personal study time, what other opportunities exist for you to study the Word?*

ACTION: Identify at least one outside opportunity for you to engage the Word with other people. This can be through your church's weekly bible study or Sunday school or even studying with friends. Commit to participating with this group for at least 6 months.

DEVELOPING A PRAYER LIFE

The last component of *Nourishing* is tied to your prayer life. While studying the word can be difficult, it is one of the more tangible elements of spiritual nourishment that exists. What has gone somewhat unacknowledged thus far is the role of prayer in this process. It is through prayer that God can reconnect or connect you with the local church. It is through prayer that God will provide you the discernment required to engage the scriptures. And ultimately, it is through prayer that God will give you the strength to walk faithfully in your journey of celibacy.

Of all the components of *Nourishing*, I found developing a prayer life the hardest. First off, it was hard because I had never been much of a "prayer." I mean, I blessed my food before I ate (most times) and would pray before a test while in school, or before performance reviews as a professional. So, in some respects I did pray, but my reasons weren't the most noble. Nonetheless, I still found it difficult because I just was not sure about what to say. As anxiety and doubt crept in, I became cynical about the value of prayer. I knew that the enemy was out to distract me and understood that these emotions were all part of the process. Yet still, I allowed his attacks to affect me until I ran across a passage of scripture during my studying of the Word (I told you they all tie together!) that encouraged me to be *anxious in nothing* and submit my requests to the Lord in prayer[1]. As a result of this new found direction as it related to prayer, I began to pray to God for calmness and protection. I prayed to Him and candidly let Him know what was on my mind. I told Him my fears and exposed my insecurities. I questioned His commands and shared my cynicism about sexual purity in the 21st century. And as I talked to Him, I found myself calming down. Once I finished, in Jesus' name, I concluded.

Often times, I'd get up from my bedside and get into the bed and just lay there in the quiet of my room. Sometimes I would stay kneeling as though I had more to say, but the words had not yet come to me. Regardless of where I was after the prayer, it was something about it that made me feel His presence. Sometimes it would be more powerful than others, but as I continued to build my prayer life I noticed that I began to feel closer to Him. This closeness was experienced in my willingness to share my mistakes without fear of repercussion, my desire to seek His forgiveness immediately in times of trouble and my stronger commitment to submit to His will for my life. As my prayer life grew, I became less self-centered and more Christ-centered. With Him at the center, much of the burden experienced earlier on in the journey began to subside. **Prayer had moved from something that I did out**

[1]   Philippians 4:6

of selfish motives to something I did out of relationship with God.

In similar fashion with studying the Word, in order to develop an authentic prayer life you will need to be disciplined. I suggest that you make prayer how you open up any and all studies of the Word. Before my daily study, I would pray to the Lord for clarity and discernment as I studied His Word. In addition to prayer as part of your study life, praying before leaving the house to get your day started and at night before you go to sleep are also highly recommended times. My pastor preached a sermon a while ago that talked about the spiritual warfare that we engage in unknowingly as we wake up and go to sleep each night. He chided us over the reality that most of us spend a large portion of our mornings grooming and spend little to no time with God; given the attacks that await you when you exit your home, this cannot be your reality. You must be prayed up in order to be prepared for the day's events. That guy or girl at work may have on your favorite cologne/ perfume today. Better yet, they may have on that outfit that makes you do multiple double-takes. Your ex may send you a text today reminiscing on the "old days" with vivid depictions to see if there's an opportunity for them to slide back in. All of these attacks await you as you prepare to begin your day. As if the celibacy journey isn't hard enough already, don't allow yourself to walk out into the world unarmed with God's grace and mercy sought out through prayer.

In addition, praying before you go to sleep is key too because of the baggage you bring back into your home from the world. Think of all of the evil, unjust acts and sadness you witness through the course of the day. Think about all of the temptations you fought during your day; the ones you fought off and the ones you succumbed to. It would be naïve to think that going to sleep will just make these things go away and so, it is critical that you pray before going to sleep in order to download the day's events, seek out repentance and free up your mind for rest and peace.

As you can see, prayer is an integral piece of the *Nourishing* phase. It is fundamental to your renewed relationship with God and it serves as the primary mode of communication. Without prayer, you run the risk of inhibiting the Spirit of God to guide and teach you as you study the Word and seek out connection with the church. Without prayer, you make yourself extremely vulnerable to the attacks of the enemy who wants nothing more than for you to fail in your walk. There's no getting around it. Prayer is key. And note: do not be intimidated by the prayers you may hear from some of today's clergy. There is no "right" way to pray other than to be authentic in your submissions to the Lord. Jesus provided us with a framework on prayer and if looking for an example of authenticity, seek His word.

In Matthew Chapter 6[1], Jesus said,

"Our Father in heaven, hallowed be your name,
your kingdom come,
your will be done, on earth as it is in heaven. Give us today
our daily bread.
And forgive us our debts, as we also have forgiven
our debtors. And lead us
not into temptation, but deliver us from
the evil one."(NIV)

It's a simple prayer and yet, it is one that embodies the essence of what every prayer should be about.

---

[1]   Matthew 6:9–13

MOMENT OF INTROSPECTION:

- *How often do you pray? What do you pray about/for?*

ACTION: Pick a time of day that will work for you to pray every day. On a calendar, count out 30 days from today and mark day 30. Commit to praying at your designated time(s) each day for 30 straight days. A mentor once told me that if you do something for 30 days it becomes a habit.

- *Are there others in your life who could use your prayers?*

ACTION: Create a prayer list of individuals who you want to pray for on a daily basis. This list will be dynamic and can change from day to day. It is a helpful tool as you will encounter different people throughout your day who may need your intercession.

Nourishing is an exciting phase because you will learn things about yourself and God. And now that you are nourished, you are prepared to enter the biggest phase of the celibate journey. As you prepare to enter the next phase, understand that the first two phases are still in progress. The process of rededication is an ever-evolving process and as you conquer one thing, God reveals a new obstacle for you to climb. Subsequently, continue to purge and nourish as you see fit and as God reveals to you in preparation for phase III, *Living*.

PHASE III: LIVING

[Living (verb)– to be alive]

*T*he last two phases focused primarily on you and your relationship with God. Phase III will focus on you and your relationships with people. It would be too easy to declare celibacy and then remain in a vacuum for the rest of your life; stowed away from life's temptations (though there are plenty of temptations present within your own mind that don't require the assistance of someone else). But, that's not what this walk is about. In today's society where sexual immorality has become a norm, God is looking for His children to step up to the plate and walk boldly. **Thus, your celibate journey cannot be a private affair because if it were, how would He be able to use you as a light in the world?**

Am I saying you have to go and present workshops on celibacy? No, not at all. But, what I am saying is that you have a responsibility to make yourself available to the people of God for His will to be done. *Purging and Nourishing* afforded you the opportunity to deal with the demons of the past and fill yourself up on the things of God. Now, *Living* requires that you plug back into the world in which we live and go out to be an example. While the responsibility might at first seem daunting, this truly is the fun part of the journey!

So, let's take a look at living from the perspective of three areas:
1. Accountability
2. Socializing
3. Dating

ACCOUNTABILITY

One of the things I found hugely beneficial in my journey was the accountability afforded by likeminded friends. If you'll recall in my story, I specifically mentioned Jason and Nneka as two friends that supported me (and I them) early on in my journey. I can't underestimate the value that accountability partners have on the journey. As I mentioned before, the journey will have its lonely days, but on those days you can count on your accountability partners to help support you. There will definitely be moments when the flesh will become weak and you will find yourself on the brink of sin. It is in those moments that your accountability partners can serve as the subtle voice(s) of God to encourage you to continue the good fight. That's their job; to hold you accountable. Though a simple task, it has everything to do with your success as you begin living again.

I understand that some of you might view your rededication to Christ and a new commitment of celibacy as a private matter. While I recognize the value of keeping the journey to yourself, let me be the first to tell you that doing so is a very risky proposition. Why? Because in isolation, there is, oftentimes, no accountability. Sure, God will continue to convict you through the Holy Spirit and this will serve as a measure of accountability. But, isn't this the same measure of accountability that you ignored for most of your life in the first place? For me it was and unfortunately, I had gotten pretty clever in my tactics to ignore this voice. However, when I surrounded myself with accountability partners, I found this approach to be much more effective as it served to augment the work of the Holy Spirit, not replace.

Where can you find accountability partners? Glad you asked! You may have already identified them during the *Purging* phase. Maybe they are the friendships that stood the test of time or maybe they are a product of the acquaintances that you promoted to friends. Better yet, maybe it's the brother or sister you met as part of the ministry at your church. No matter their origins, know that **God's process of restoration will position you in such a way that you will have people around you who can support** you in this respect. While he will do that part, it will be your job to engage them and share your journey. This is why, again, it is imperative that as you begin the process of *Living*, you remove any inhibitions you may have regarding the privacy of your journey.

So, how does the accountability partnership work? Well, first off, my partners would check-in with me multiple times during the week and especially on weekends. One key element to the accountability relationship is transparency. If I was going out on a date, I gave them a heads-up. When I got back from that date, I gave them a recap. It may sound childish, but the reality for me was that I didn't trust myself enough early on to just do these things in the dark without someone else knowing. As a result, I allowed my accountability partners the opportunity to be aware of what was going on with me at all times and thus, put them in the position to know what prayers to pray and when to pray them (this is key!) for me as I continued on my journey. Additionally, because they knew everything that was going on, I was even more challenged to go against God's will. Why? Because I knew that I would soon be speaking with them and I did not want to be compelled to lie. After all, we were friends who had made a covenant of accountability with one another. Dishonesty would not have been a good way to honor this.

Lastly, it is preferred that these accountability partners are committed to the same journey to which you are holding yourself accountable. It would be somewhat disingenuous for someone who's not celibate to hold you accountable. Sure, it's possible that someone who's still sexually active can check up on you and make sure you're continuing in your commitment to God. But, the problem will arise when you find yourself struggling. They will not be able to relate to this struggle and thus, their advice or guidance may come ill-advised due to lack of understanding. As a result, seek out accountability partners who are down for the cause and willing to walk with you as you pursue a life of sexual purity.

MOMENT OF INTROSPECTION:

- *Who do you know that you can ask to become your accountability partner(s)?*

ACTION: Write out a list of guidelines that you and your partners will use to govern the partnership. Such as: How often will you speak? Will you study the Word together? How often? Will you engage in corporate prayer together? If so, how often? Can you contact one another at any time or are there "forbidden times?"

- *What do you feel represents your biggest area of weakness that an accountability partner can help you with?*

SOCIALIZING (*re-introduction into society*)

With your accountability partners on deck, it's now time to begin socializing again. As part of the purging process, you probably found yourself abstaining from a lot of environments that contained people and things that represented the old you in order to prevent relapse. Well, now that you've purged and thoroughly nourished, you are prepared to re-engage these environments without that same fear. One of the big questions that will come up during *Purging* as you eliminate and refrain from some activities in your life will be, "Why?" What I found, is that this question is usually asked from a position of right or wrong. For example, I stopped going to clubs and thus, my friends wanted to know why. Were the clubs inherently wrong? Honestly, in my opinion, I don't think there is much good that can come from going to a club. Especially for me as a man who is now married. With the abundance of alcohol consumption and scantily clad women (no offense...), I struggle to come up with a justification that will suit God and my wife for why I need to be there. Even as a single during my journey, for the very same reasons, I struggled to come up with an "out" for God in order to begin going again frivolously.

That said, there were some specific instances where I did go to clubs again post-*Purging* during my celibate journey. As an example, in one instance, one of my friends invited me out to catch up and he wanted to go by this club that his friends were at. In another instance, one of my close friends was having a birthday party at a club. When I first seriously committed to celibacy, I would not have gone to the club in either of these instances because I was still too new to the journey and too vulnerable to the very sin I was trying to avoid. But, at the time that these two instances occurred, I had already gone through my purging and nourishing phases and I was now living. Not living in the "I'm grown and I can do what I want sense," but living in the sense that I was fully alive in my walk. I had studied the Word deeply, I had established a strong prayer life and I had accountability partners who had my back. My mind had truly been renewed and my motives reset. As a result, I had grown more confident in my celibate walk and I was no longer as vulnerable to the things of the world. For this reason, I was able to go to the club in these two instances and not fall victim to the vices within the club (NOTE: I went to the club because they asked/requested, not because I wanted to). The desire to go to clubs at this point had been taken away through the restorative process. If the desire had still been there, I would not have gone because that would have been a sign that this "known vice" was still an area that I needed God's help to purge. However, please understand that it took some time for me to get to this point and if I were not comfortable, I would not have gone. Ultimately, the pace by which one can begin living again will vary from person to person, so you will have to make this decision for yourself (not under the compulsion of any outside influence). As you begin living, you will learn to strike a balance with what it means to *be in the world, but not of the world*[1].

The *Living* phase is about just that; living. And part of living is being social and a part of society. While there was a time where disengaging society was part of the redemptive process and necessary for you to land in a position to be restored, now is the time for you to live and be free in Christ. God wants to get the glory out of the changes that He has made within you. He wants you to be exposed to those same people who knew you in the most sinful of days so that they can inquire about the change in you. It is in that inquisition that God's glory has an opportunity to be seen. Just like in the instances I highlighted above regarding the club, you too have an opportunity through living and socializing to be a light in darkness. In doing this, always remember to keep the earlier principles in mind as you live. Study and prayer are two things learned during *Nourishing* that will help to keep you humble and of pure mindset as you live. The worst thing you can do is to begin living and then stop nourishing. The two go hand in hand and in order to experience the joy available to you by

---

[1]   John 17:13–19

living, you must continue to keep Christ at the center of your life!

MOMENT OF INTROSPECTION:

- *What is your biggest fear associated with socializing?*

- *Do you feel that you are strong enough to fully "re-enter" society? If not, why? Are there things in Phase I that you need to revisit before moving forward?*

ACTION: Create an action plan for your re-introduction into society. Be sure to include the role that your accountability partners will play as well as a schedule of activities from Nourishing that you will continue to do.

DATING

As I began the phase of Living in my own journey, I was deeply challenged by my new awareness of what was allowable; ultimately foreplay would be out of play for this journey. As I continued to seek God's will and began to socialize, oddly enough, the dating scene became unfamiliar to me. Not that the locations I would go to in an attempt to meet women had changed, but all of a sudden I felt uncomfortable. I began to view women in a different light and quite honestly, was embarrassed at my past dating explorations. See, in all my years I had not learned how to date God's way. With the objective of sex (and all things considered sexual) gone, I did not know where to begin. I was like a toddler trying to form coherent sentences. It took some time, but through the continued process of Nourishing, God began to reveal to me how to date in a manner that would be pleasing to Him.

Today, as a society, we have subconsciously trivialized the act of dating. Dating in its purest sense really is courtship. Unfortunately, we've bastardized the term courtship because of its serious overtone. Webster's defines courting as: to engage in social activities leading to engagement and marriage. That's serious stuff right? But, let's be real for a second. The majority of us (the mature) look at individuals we date along the lines of whether or not they could be a suitable mate. Sure, we may have no intention of marrying them in the near future or even committing to them in a boyfriend/girlfriend (or insert favorite relationship designation here) type of way, but the thought crosses our mind. After all, we are giving that person one of the most valuable gifts we have...our time. So, in all honesty, mentally there is already an unacknowledged seriousness to dating that is important to note. Thus, let me make a suggestion. From here on out, replace dating with courting in your vernacular; this will be a first step towards eliminating the casualness associated with dating. Not surprisingly, in my own life, it was this same casualness that made me most vulnerable to sexual immorality.

Now, from God's perspective, if we are to uphold his principles, then dating must have two key components: *God* and *Purpose*. Though this may seem light and trite, as I reflect on my own experiences I am amazed at how many dating situations I found myself in that lacked both! So, what does it mean to have God and Purpose in a dating situation? Let's take a look at each one separately.

Presence of *God* in Dating

To have God in a dating situation means that **God is at the center!** Not to the right. Not to the left. Right in the center. But, for **God to be in the center** there is a level of personal preparation that must occur first and foremost; i.e. Nourishing. Far too many times we jump into situations with other people full of confidence before we are even ready ourselves. Thus, the *Nourishing* phase is critical and imperative for anyone who seeks to date God's way. This time of preparation will allow you to develop a more intimate relationship with the Father – one that will serve to guard and protect you against the enemy in times of despair. There are really four tenets to abide by during personal preparation:

1. **Fellowship with believers** – It is important that you take advantage of this time to become acquainted with the assembly of believers as they will become a source of friendship and ultimately provide you with a support system. A word of caution: Be sure that these believers are sincerely attempting to walk in the Spirit, and not just to laying on God's grace.

2. **Study the Word of God** – Studying the Word of God daily will increase your discernment, provide you with examples of godly relationships and teach you God's commands so that you will know what obedience means.

3. **Develop a good prayer life** – This component may pose as an ambiguous principle, but it is critical

to any amount of personal preparation because it is what serves as the foundation of an intimate relationship with God. Remember that prayer is simply communicating honestly with God (that means speaking AND listening!)

4. **Identify an accountability partner** – An accountability partner will help you to stay on the right path and through a transparent relationship, will promote humility and serve as a springboard for some of the more sensitive issues you may encounter. It is strongly advised that this accountability partner be someone of the same sex.

It is my belief that if you have been diligent in the four tenets above in the context of the three phases of the journey, you are now in a position to date God's way. For my sisters, this position is often perceived as sitting and waiting. The beauty of that position, if you have focused on the four tenets, is that you will be surrounded by believers who have now become friends, filled with God's word, developed an intimate relationship with the Father and have an accountability partner that you can trust and confide in. Trust me; it will be very difficult for a Bozo to slip through the cracks with this type of foundation! For my brothers, if you have faithfully done the above, then it is now time to practice one of them in praying to God for guidance on when and who to date. I know that you were ready to run and exude your swagger toward the next woman that crossed your path. However, if you do this, you would have already abandoned component number one of dating God's way – God himself! But don't fret, as by this time your relationship with God will be at a level that you will be able to trust in Him, His timing, and His will and not become weary in well doing[1] in your quest to date God's way.

Presence of *Purpose* in Dating

So, you're prepared and you've sought God's face on him/her (that's right, ladies even when he approaches you, you should immediately take it up with the Father to seek his will, not yours, first!), so what's next? You're almost ready for the first date, but we need to take a second to discuss the last key component of dating God's way – Purpose.

See, dating as we treat it today allows us to engage in social activities just for the fun of doing it, but courting by definition calls us to a higher responsibility in that of a **purpose**. So, dating God's way really becomes courting, meaning that if I am dating God's way, I am engaging in social activities with the purpose of engagement or marriage.

---

1   Galatians 6:9

Dating God's way is not the frivolous, non-committal activity that society has taught us, but it is an activity that has behind it a true and sincere **purpose**. Now, does that mean that by courting someone you will automatically become engaged? Absolutely not, but your purpose for the activities is to see if that is on the horizon. And the good thing about courtship is that there is open communication. Neither party should be left wondering what is going on in the situation. With God at the center, the man should be comfortable stating his intentions and the woman her expectations. This may seem like a bit much for our current society. If that is the thought that is running through your mind right now, I don't blame you. But, aren't you tired of trying it your way? Has your way produced the results you've been seeking? If not, give God's way a shot and I promise you that you will not be disappointed.

Ultimately, dating God's way, if done faithfully, will be one of the most rewarding experiences you will ever have. Many of your friends and close associates may find it to be weird and question you, but you have to remain focused on your spiritual duty. Dating God's way is not intended to take the fun and excitement out of meeting that special someone, but it is intended to cause us to be more responsible in that search. That responsibility calls us to a higher, more Godly standard of living – one in which our light is able to be seen in this dark world. We must remember that just as in the Garden of Eden, God sets boundaries for our protection and well-being. Not to stifle us or make us miserable, but to benefit us beyond our limited sight. When we try things the way God designed them to be, we find peace, joy, and fulfillment that is far greater than that which the world consistently advertises. My courtship that led to marriage bears witness to this very fact. I know that if I had not learned how to do things God's way I would have never been prepared to receive the woman God placed in my life to be my helpmate. It has truly been a blessing to build with her as we now collectively seek God's will for our lives each day. With that, here are a few tips for your first date that will be sure to keep **God at the center** of your dating situation and ensure a *purposeful* experience. Enjoy!

Tips for the "First Date"

1. **Allow God a seat at the table** – Make sure that you engage God in your dating situation so that you are able to make informed decisions about when and who. You do not want to end up in a situation where things go awry and you have not once brought the person or the situation to God to seek His will.

2. **Set your Boundaries** – This is about as key as it gets. Paul said in Corinthians that everything is

permissible, but not everything is beneficial[1]. With *God at the center*, you will be able to openly discuss your boundaries without fear of compromise.

3. **Expose him/her to your faith** – Assuming that you've followed the other steps, this should not be necessary, as they should know well before the date that you are a child of God. But, what is also equally important is that you continue to keep God and the faith exposed throughout the relationship. The enemy does not need much room to sneak in and cause disruption.

4. **Maintain sexual purity** – In the absence of sexual purity, the other three items become moot points and the first date can become a spiritual disaster. However, if God is at the center and there is purpose, God will honor your efforts and come alongside you in maintaining sexual purity.

---

[1]   1 corinthinas 6:12

MOMENT OF INTROSPECTION:

- *Do you feel that you are ready to date? Why?*

- *Men: Are you willing to allow God to guide your steps in dating?*

- *Women: Are you willing to wait on God's timing, not your own as it relates to dating?*

ACTION: On a sheet of paper, create four columns. In the first, write out a list of characteristics of your ideal man or woman. In the second, explain why each characteristic is important to you. In the third, write either "Yes" or "No" for whether or not this characteristic is important to God. In the fourth, explain your answer from the third column. Sum up the Yes' and No's and reflect on any disconnects that may exist.

APPENDIX :
WHY CELIBACY?

*W*hen I became celibate, the one question that I heard often was, "why are you celibate?" Sometimes it would be asked in sincerity and other times sarcastically. And as much as this inquiry annoyed me in the initial days and months of my walk, I came to realize that it was a very legitimate question. Legitimate because not everyone is a Christian (or anything else for that matter). Legitimate because, although a Christian, I myself was sexually active with little remorse for a considerable portion of my adult life. Legitimate because there are many churches that do not deal with the issue of sexual immorality head-on and leave it to parenting and/or "maturity." It appears that they assume that most young adults will just figure out how to deal with it. So, with these observations, it's no wonder why someone would ask the question of why. Well, the answer to this question lies in the Word of God.

The following scripture served as the foundation for me as I sought to understand what celibacy meant:

1 Corinthians 6:12-20:

> 12"Everything is permissible for me"—but not everything is beneficial. "Everything is permissible for me"—but I will not be mastered by anything. 13"Food for the stomach and the stomach for food"—but God will destroy them both. The body is not meant for sexual immorality, but for the Lord, and the Lord for the body. 14By his power God raised the Lord from the dead, and he will raise us also. 15Do you not know that your bodies are members of Christ himself? Shall I then take the members of Christ and unite them with a prostitute? Never! 16Do you not know that he who unites himself with a prostitute is one with her in body? For it is said, "The two will become one flesh." 17But he who unites himself with the Lord is one with him in spirit. 18Flee from sexual immorality. All other sins a man commits are outside his body, but he who sins sexually sins against his own body. 19Do you not know that your body is a temple of the Holy Spirit, who is in you, whom you have received from God? You are not your own; 20you were bought at a price. Therefore honor God with your body." (NIV)

This Corinthians text is truly one of my favorites in the Bible because it contains so much value in each and every sentence. For a quick backdrop, Paul is writing to the Corinthian church in response to some issues they were having as an early church and one issue in particular – moral laxness. Underneath this moral laxness lied sexual immorality and other misinterpretations of permissibility within their newly developed Christian faith. But, before going into further exegesis, I want to focus in on the bolded portions of this great pericope to uncover the rationale behind celibacy for our practical use today.

Being a member of the body of Christ comes at a cost. There is an age old debate amongst theologians around free will, but the reality is that once you become a Christian there are some things that you will choose not to do anymore because of the unction of the Holy Spirit within. Now, while the Holy Spirit is working to renew your mind, there will still be some activities and behaviors that have not been dealt with and the first sentence in the Corinthians text deals with those things. Sure, everything is permissible. But, everything is not beneficial. In an effort not to relegate our belief in Jesus and our subsequent salvation down to a ton of do's and don'ts, it is important to understand what Paul is telling us. If you truly believe in Jesus and that He died on an old rugged cross for your sins, then out of love there are some things you should choose not to do because you love Him. There are some things that will not be beneficial as it relates to growing closer with Christ. See, I consider it a blessing that God convicted me around my sexual immorality because prior to that, my actions did not reflect someone who loved their Savior. How do I know? I still run into people today who are amazed that I was celibate and will make statements like "Oh, you found Jesus" or "you on that church kick now huh?" In reality, these statements are embarrassing to me because I had found Him a long time ago, but unfortunately, I allowed myself to revel in non-beneficial things for too long.

"...Everything is permissible for me"—but I will not be mastered by anything." – 1 Corinthians 6:12 (NIV)

The second part of the 1st verse bolded here in the text seems a bit redundant, but Paul adds an additional condition to his previous point. What does it mean to be mastered by something? I would gesture to say that many of us at times have allowed ourselves to be mastered by sex. For men, we often fall under the spell of sex via the urging of the male braggadocio and become recklessly focused on it. We become so obsessed with it that we will say and do any and everything to obtain it. In addition, a key indication of its mastery over us is our willingness to compromise. This can often be seen with women. Traditionally, women are more "values-driven" and society allows them to express their values without oppression. While these values are expressed outwardly, it is this proclamation that often gets compromised when it comes to sex. For example, a woman who desires a man may find herself fighting with her spiritual obligation of celibacy as a consequence of this very desire. The world teaches women that without sex, finding a partner will be nearly impossible.

As a result, compromise becomes a way of life and thus, sex or the acquiescence thereof becomes ones master due to its manipulative ability.

"...The body is not meant for sexual immorality, but for the Lord, and the Lord for the body." – 1 Corinthians 6:13 (NIV)

The next verse that I've highlighted points out a truth that was far from my consciousness when I pursued sex with reckless abandon. Sure, I knew that the body was not for sexual immorality (although I didn't act as such), but what always puzzled me was the question of what then should the body be used for. In this sentence, Paul makes it plain – for the Lord. I have to admit that at first, I did not know what this really meant. But, as I began to walk in purity, I came to a clearer understanding of this passage. In essence, the full function of my body belongs to the Lord. It's that simple. Whenever I'm doing something that is not aligned with that, I'm using my body out of the context that God had intended from the beginning. I found this particularly powerful because as I began introspectively evaluating my own motivations behind my sexual perversion, I came to realize that the root of my issue was selfishness. I had carried myself in a manner as though this body that I have was for me and my fulfillment. I didn't owe anyone anything, and as a result, sexual immorality was one of the ways that I found fulfillment. But, once I realized and internalized that my body was for the Lord, I realized that I would have to become unselfish. I would have to deny myself in order to be in His will. That denial of self first manifested itself as passing on dates with women after certain times of nights. It showed up as my restrictions around having women stay overnight at my house. These things, though simple, were the very things I did in the past to please myself. And as I pursued self-denial, I realized that self-denial for self-denial sake would not be a sustainable lifestyle. That said, I came to understand that these activities that I used to enjoy would need to be immediately replaced with the things of God. As a result, I sought out opportunities within my church to be of service to the body of Christ. As I immersed myself in various ministries within the church, I began to find self-denial much less difficult and found solace in the fact that I had finally begun to use my body for the Lord.

"Flee from sexual immorality." – 1 Corinthians 6:18 (NIV)

Flee from sexual immorality! Notice Paul's aggressive language here. He doesn't say to walk away from or passively dodge it, but he says to flee. When I think of the word flee, I imagine a criminal running from the police or a child running from a stray dog. In both instances, the person fleeing is doing so without haste and in effect, trying to spare themselves from harm or consequence. This one verse, more than the others, truly provides practical guidance. When I first committed to the Lord that I would follow his command and strive for celibacy, I did so ignorantly. I did it without acknowledging the power of the enemy. One of the devil's biggest attacks on God's people, especially teens and young adults, is that of sex. Once I made the decision to claim victory in the Lord's name in this area of my life, the devil began an aggressive pursuit to get me to backslide. He tempted me by throwing women of the past at me (those that I wanted to have sex with, but it never materialized), he frustrated me by bringing women in my life who scoffed at the idea of celibacy and he even had members of clergy (men) look at me in bewilderment when I shared with them the choice I made. All of these things put chinks in my spiritual armor and for a period of time, weakened my stance. But as I meditated on this scripture, I realized that being celibate would not be easy. I would have to literally run from it; not just the act itself, but also the external influences that had the potential to drive me back into the bed. As such, I recognized the attempts of the devil as what they were and turned my back on him. Not only did I turn my back, but I pursued God even more because I knew that I would only find resolve in His word. It was my pursuit of Him even more that allowed me to prevail over the devil's attempts.

"Do you not know that your body is a temple of the Holy Spirit, who is in you..." – 1 Corinthians 6:19 (NIV)

The next verse really hit home for me. It's similar to the earlier point around one's body being for the Lord, however, this sentence highlights that our bodies are truly the temple of the Holy Spirit. That's deep. When we accept Christ, he makes a deposit in us. The Holy Spirit is that deposit so that His presence is always with us to guide and protect. However, oftentimes, we allow ourselves to get so disconnected from God, that the Holy Spirit's voice in our lives is faint. When you think about the fact that your body is in fact the temple of the Holy Spirit, it changes your perspective on what you do with it and where you take it. With this awareness, I was able to establish boundaries that would prove beneficial in my journey. As a result, I sought out to make sure that I did not take the Holy Spirit to places or put it in situations that were not edifying to God. In those moments where I would find myself weak, I would think back on this particular part of the text to find strength and direction on choices contemplated.

"...you were bought at a price. Therefore honor God with your body."- 1 Corinthians 6:20 (NIV)

The last bolded verse is probably the most important of them all. When I felt dejected due to my choice to follow God in this area of my life, when none of the other parts of this text brought me comfort, it was this last verse that really humbled me. This life that I live...it's not mine. My salvation was bought at a price! Jesus died for my sins at Calvary. The least I could do was honor God with my body. It's true, for all that Christ had done, is doing and will do in my life, the least I could/can do is honor Him with my body. Every day I wake up is a blessing from God. Every time I get in my car and make it safely to my destination is a blessing from God. I owe Him everything! So, no matter how hard the journey was, I had to always remember that I was bought at price...

In addition to the Corinthians text, I also found Colossians 3:1-7 and Romans 12:1-2 very helpful as I sought God's word on my newly adopted lifestyle.

Colossians 3:1-7:

1Since, then, you have been raised with Christ, set your hearts on things above, where Christ is seated at the right hand of God. 2Set your minds on things above, not on earthly things.3For you died and your life is now hidden with Christ in God. 4When Christ, who is your life, appears, then you also will appear with him in glory.

5Put to death, therefore, whatever belongs to your earthly nature: sexual immorality, impurity, lust, evil desires and greed, which is idolatry. 6Because of these, the wrath of God is coming. 7You used to walk in these ways, in the life you once lived." (NIV)

Romans 12:1-2:

1Therefore, I urge you, brothers, in view of God's mercy, to offer your bodies as living sacrifices, holy and pleasing to God—this is your spiritual act of worship. 2Do not conform any longer to the pattern of this world, but be transformed by the renewing of your mind. Then you will be able to test and approve what God's will is—his good, pleasing and perfect will." (NIV)

Now that we've reviewed the scriptural context of celibacy, you should have a foundation from which to use during your journey. As I've mentioned numerous times before, the journey will be challenging and you will reach points of impasse from time to time. But, knowing and holding on to God's word is one way to ensure that you do not allow Satan room to fully exploit you in moments of weakness.

Here are additional scriptures to use throughout your journey: *Romans 8:5-8; 2 Corinthians 5:16-21; Galatians 5:13-26; Ephesians 4:17-24; 1 Thessalonians 4:3-8; James 4:4-10.*

ABOUT THE AUTHOR

$\mathcal{2}$ Corinthians 5:17 states, "Therefore, if anyone is in Christ, he is a new creation; the old has gone, the new has come!" It is this scripture that best characterizes the journey that Armond Mosley has taken over the past 20 years. In the summer of 2004, God began to press Armond on the issue of sexual sin. While he tried to fight this nudging of the Lord initially, it was not long before he conceded to God's will and rededicated his life to Christ and vowed to remain celibate until marriage. It was in the midst of this journey that Armond developed a more intimate relationship with the Lord and as a result, he was inspired to share his story with others, hence *Rededication* was born.

Armond is very passionate about the relationship that young adults (18-35) have with Christ. In his own life he has seen the impact that being disconnected from the kingdom can have and as a result, he founded Kingdom Workshops, LLC in order to educate, motivate and activate other young adults to fulfill the purpose(s) that God has planted in them. Through Kingdom Workshops, Armond has had the opportunity to work with many churches and universities to bring awareness to the issues facing young adults of today. Through candor, transparency and humor, Armond challenges workshop attendees to yield to the voice of God in their own lives to secure the joy that has been promised to them. Some of the signature workshop offerings are: "Dating God's Way," "God's Will vs. My Will," "Singleness as a Gift," "Single and Celibate," and "What Men Really Want." For more information, visit www.kingdomworskhops.com or e-mail info@kingdomworkshops.com.

Born to Mr. & Mrs. Alfonso Mosley, Armond is a native of Huntsville, AL who currently resides in the suburbs of Philadelphia with his wife Nneka. A graduate of Howard University and Temple University, Armond enjoys reading, watching sports and spending time with family and friends. He and Nneka serve as members of Enon Tabernacle Baptist Church in Philadelphia under the leadership of Rev. Dr. Alyn E. Waller, Senior Pastor.

ACKNOWLEDGMENTS

I have truly been humbled by this entire publication process. First, I'd like to express my gratitude and thanksgiving to my Lord and Savior, Jesus Christ, who is the head of my life. It was His grace and mercy that covered me during my journey and allowed me to get to this point. To my wife, Nneka, I thank you for being my biggest cheerleader. There were many nights where the enemy attempted to instill doubt in me regarding this project and as my God ordained helpmate, you served to shield me from his advances in those moments when I was weak. I love you dearly and thank God for blessing me with you as my wife. To my parents, Alfonso and Prence Mosley, thank you, thank you, thank you! While I know some of what you've read in this story may be "news" to you (lol!), I'm thankful that you provided me with the spiritual foundation early in life that ultimately served as the catalyst back to Christ. Daddy, you modeled for me what it meant to be a man and though I didn't quite get it right the first go around, because of your example I had something to strive towards. Mama, your patience and support have always kept me conscious of what love truly means. To Pastor Lou, if it weren't for you, I wouldn't have come to fully acknowledge the gift that God had placed in my life in that of Nneka when I did. Thank you! And also, thank you for your spiritual guidance, mentorship and friendship over the years. Minister Glenn Wilson, you've truly been a godsend since the day we first met! Your coaching and support were integral in my journey. To my boys, LeMarcus Hemphill, Brandon Jones, Kwaku Gyabaah, Jaha Howard, Byron Marshall and Gregory Stewart, thank you. You were all there for some, if not all, parts of my journey and I thank you all for being supportive of me as I began to make a transition in my life. I admire each of you and continue to cherish our friendships today. To my homegirls, Naima Harmon and Bianca Lee, thanks for being a sounding board for this project and providing me with constructive criticism from the female point of view. You've both been patient with me! To my publishing team, Godzchild Publications (www. godzchildproductions.net)... THANK YOU! Just a few months ago, I sat in my office with manuscript in hand and no idea of how I would bring this finished work to print. And then, God moved (Shout-out to Jennifer Lucy, *Dried Tears: A Woman's Guide to Overcoming*)! It has been a great pleasure working with you and I look forward to our next project together. Thanks for being a teacher and also a friend in the publishing process. Lastly, to my publication partners!! YOU HAVE TRULY BEEN A BLESSING!! And so, I'd like to give a special thanks to the following people whose financial contributions made this book possible:

Alfonso and Prence Mosley, Edward and Helena Hurley, Jaha and Vanessa Howard, Conrod and Joy Kelly, Jeff and Angela Tennessen, Naima Harmon, Selena McKnight, Kwaku and Samantha Gyabaah, Ikemefuna Udeze, Harold Allen, Reggie and Angela Jones, Levi Barnes, Genea Lee, Lincoln and Fredonia Williams, LeMarcus and Janah Hemphill, Gareth and Tara Murray, Kyle Bacon, Chambre Malone, Jon and Kim Hinton, Tamika Baxley, Ruby and Sonya LaGrand, Nashira Wallace, Tiffany Gainer, Ngozi Motilewa, Brandon Jones, Chris Thomas, Damien Carter, LaKisha D. Smith, Joshua Mercer, Chrishawn Mitchell, Chaundra Magwood, Kurt and Bronwyn Callands, Karee Payton, Cassius and Jackie Priestly, Glenn and Karen Wilson, Tiffany Battle, Rakeisha Gonzalez, Donnell Sheppard, Lee and Valerie King, April Brown, Alex Dixon, Teniece Thurston, Julian Jones, Steven Wilson, Jennifer Simmons, Lauren Holland, Patrice Clark and Tiffany McCoy.

And a very special thanks to all of those who supported me up until the 11th hour. Although I wasn't able to mention you by name, God knows your name and I am forever grateful!

Last, but not least, I want to thank you, the reader, for your support. I pray that whatever led you to this book, God has used it to add more unto you and increase your faith in Him. God Bless!!